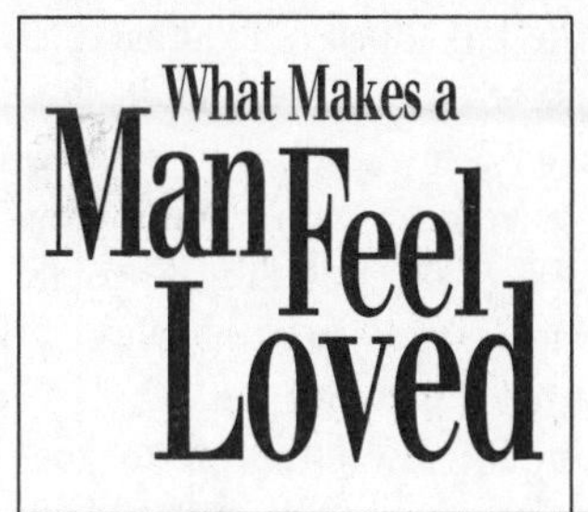

A Personal Note from the Author

Did you look twice when you saw that a man wrote this book? Are you wondering, *Why does he think he can write a book of encouragement for women? Shouldn't a woman be writing this book? After all, she would know how hard it is to be a wife!* Those are valid questions, but let's consider a different perspective.

As a man, I know what makes a man feel loved and supported. I know what men need to feel confident and appreciated. I know the inner fears and questions a man lives with. I know the frustrations a man experiences in his various roles as breadwinner, disciplinarian, handyman, car-repair expert, and spider killer. Simply put, I know how men tick—and that information can help you come alongside and support your husband. But there are other reasons why I believe I have an important message for you.

I Have Been Schooled by a Wonderful Wife

For 42 years I have been married to a woman who has truly stood by me. Emilie has shown me the patience of Job, the wisdom of Solomon, the forgiveness of Jesus, and the straightforwardness of Paul in her relationship to me. A very capable person in her own right and busy with her own areas of ministry, Emilie has always worked toward the long-term goal of helping me become the man God wants me to be.

Emilie has loved, encouraged, challenged, motivated, inspired, and supported me in every endeavor. She has stood by me, backing my ideas and my leadership even when she has had some doubts. When I have been wrong, Emilie has offered encouragement rather than chastisement, scolding, "I told you so," or the silent treatment. All through our years of marriage, I have been strengthened by her unwavering respect for me.

Emilie has always prayed for me daily. I know her prayers have changed the course of my life. Many times when I kissed her good-bye as I left for work, I would mention my 10:30 A.M. meeting with the president of Company X or my 3:30 P.M. meeting with the staff. Then, at 10:30 and 3:30, I knew the confidence that came from knowing that I had a faithful prayer warrior lifting me up before the Lord.

Through the years, Emilie's prayers have also placed a protective hedge around my heart. Knowing that she would be in prayer for me has helped protect me from feelings of anger, resentment, defeat, or egotism. Whenever I was away from the family at a convention, I knew that Emilie was praying for my safety, purity, obedience to God's Word, and protection from Satan's attacks. Also, being so in tune with God and with me, Emilie—like many intuitive wives—has often been aware of my needs before I've been aware of them myself. Finally, as a woman of prayer, Emilie is someone I can turn to with every decision that needs to be made, confident that her perspective will be godly and wise.

Emilie has also made me a hero to our children, Jennifer and Bradley, and to our grandchildren: Christine, Chad, Bevan, Bradley Joe, and Westin. She has always made it a priority to teach them to support my leadership, appreciate me in word and deed, and respectfully acknowledge my role in the family. Just as Emilie has taught me what a gift a godly wife can be, she can undoubtedly teach you as I share from my experience as her husband.

I HAVE BEEN TAUGHT BY GOD'S WORD

Through the years, I have studied the Bible—both the Old and New Testaments—to see what God teaches men and women about marriage, children, and family. Even as a very young man I wanted to mirror, to the best of my ability, God's principles for being a man, a husband, and a father. My desire has always been for my life, marriage, and family to reflect what God teaches. While I'm still in the

This book is dedicated to my wife, Emilie, and to all women who have hung in there when the going got rough. You are truly the ones who have found favor with God.

It isn't easy to persevere when you can't see the light at the end of the tunnel. But as survivors, you are a witness to the world of God's love and His abounding grace. You are proof that those who believe the principles and promises of Scripture—no matter what the situation—will later reap the blessings that accompany them.

Through every circumstance you trusted God, prayed with great fervor, and clung to that man you took in marriage. May we men become as committed to our marriage and family as you, our wives, are!

I thank God each day for the precious wife He has given me. I am the man I am today because of my God and my wife. Emilie has made this book possible. Without her, I never would have written these thoughts on paper.

Thank you, Emilie, for standing by me when you have felt like quitting!

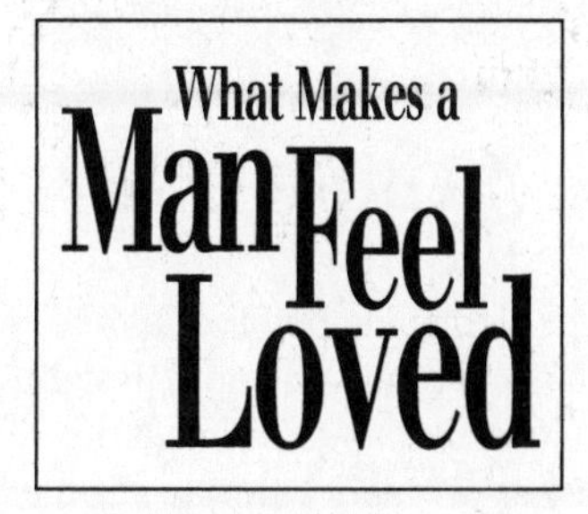

Contents

FOREWORD

When God made Bob Barnes, the mold was broken. He is a unique, talented, insightful, and discerning man. I have to laugh a bit when I say that because my Bob has an identical twin brother. Even though they do look alike, they are each so different in a lot of ways and similar in others.

My Bob and I met on a blind date over 42 years ago, never realizing the significant task that marriage would be. We were starry-eyed and ready to begin a loving relationship for life. When the rough times came, and they did, we attempted to follow God's principles with the help of family, Christian friends, and our church family. We walked through those rough times and were refined by them.

What my Bob will share with you through the pages of this book has worked for us, and will help you to see your marriage from your husband's perspective. You will gain insights into your man and discover why he may see life through a different set of lenses than you do. You might also come to better understand why your mate seems so different or even weird at times!

My Bob and I have worked together in our ministry, More Hours in My Day, since 1982. Each year we meet thousands of women just like you, who have teachable spirits and want the best relationships possible with their men. Through these encounters my Bob has felt your heartbeat, and he is sensitive to your desires and needs for an intimate relationship with your husband.

The words you're about to read come from a man who loves God and wants to encourage us as wives to support, love and help our husbands become better men.

Let my Bob touch your heart as he has mine.

—Emilie Barnes

process of becoming all that God wants me to be as a person, husband, and father, I have had ample opportunities to test the Bible's principles in the laboratory of life, and I have found them to be sound. In this book, I'll be sharing with you what I have learned.

I Have Listened to You

Since 1982, I have worked with Emilie in our More Hours in My Day ministry. At our seminars, I have listened to and spoken with thousands of women across the country. Wherever Emilie and I go—California or New York, Texas or Michigan—women have the same concerns, questions, and desires for their men, their marriages, and their families.

- How can I get my husband to communicate with me?
- Why won't my husband share how he feels?
- What can I do to encourage my husband to be the leader in our family?
- How can I respect my husband?
- Why is he so involved in his job?
- Do men really have fragile egos?
- The children hardly know their father, and they don't understand him at all. How can I get the kids and their dad together?
- How do I love a husband who isn't a Christian?
- Are men really different from women?
- I know we loved each other when we were married, but I'm not sure we do now.
- What does a man want in a woman? In a wife?
- How can I make myself more attractive to my man?

I've heard you raise these issues and ask these questions, and I have some answers to share.

I Know the Hope of the Lord

My heart is burdened by the many families I see that are separated and hurting because one or both spouses aren't willing to examine what God says about the sacred institution of marriage and come under the authority of biblical teaching. I am saddened by the women I've seen who have given up on their men too soon and made decisions about their marriage that are contrary to God's Word. At the same time, I am encouraged by what I've seen God do to revitalize marriages. I want to share with you the hope we can have in the Lord—especially if you are running low on hope for your marriage and family.

Throughout this book I've sprinkled some wise and thought-provoking quotes to encourage you in your marriage relationship. My hope is that these will bring cheer to your day and enrich your life.

So why am I writing this book? Because I can offer you a unique and valuable look at marriage from a male perspective. I have learned much about marriage in my 42 years as a husband, and I have studied the scriptural guidelines that God gives for a fulfilling marriage and family. I have tested those principles and I trust them. I also know the concerns women have about their husbands, and I have hope in the grace of our Lord. I have seen Him bring new life to stale marriages, distant husbands, and weary wives. So hang in there! In the strength of the Lord and with the guidance of His Word, you can improve your marriage and help your man become all that God designed him to be.

Bob Barnes

What Makes a Man Feel Loved

1

Overcoming the Lies Around Us

If any of you lacks wisdom, he should ask God, who gives generously to all without finding fault, and it will be given to him.

—James 1:5 NIV

Somewhere between the thrill of the engagement, the hectic preparation for the wedding, and the joy of The Big Day—and often despite excellent premarital counseling—the message gets lost, overlooked, or silenced. That message? Marriage is hard work.

Even in the best of circumstances, the demands of daily life and the hours one or both spouses work outside the home take their toll on the marriage relationship. Friends and lovers become business partners and virtual strangers. Children become the main topic of conversation and the primary focus of prayers. Older parents need care, bills need to be paid, the Sunday school program needs teachers, and the lawn needs mowing. Energy is gone long before the day is over, and the day is over long before the "to do" list is complete. Even with the Lord as the foundation, marriage is hard work.

The Way of the World

And marriage is made even harder these days by the world's view of men, women, marriage, and the family. What the world preaches certainly isn't what God had in mind when He made us in His image, instituted marriage, and declared it good!

The Scriptures clearly teach that God created Eve from Adam's rib so that she could be Adam's helpmate (Genesis 2:18). Today's society, however, slams the door on that truth. While it's good that women have made some important and long overdue strides toward social, political, and economic equality, some women, unfortunately, have pushed for equality to the point of erasing the distinctive differences God created in men and women so they could complement one another. Some have even gone so far as to say, "Who needs men?" In response, many men have become passive, quiet, and unsure about their role in relation to women. In fact, they have no idea what God intends them to be, and women are frustrated because their men aren't meeting their needs in the marriage and the family. Women cry out to their husbands, "Get with the program!" and the men softly ask, "What program?" Men and women alike have strayed from God's design for marriage, and as a result, are at odds with their mates.

Lies We are Told

Conflicts between husbands and wives are often triggered by certain ideas that society tells women to believe about themselves and about men. In fact, clinical psychologist and author Dr. Toni Grant points out ten lies that the modern "liberated" woman has bought into—lies based on the false promises propagated by the more extreme elements of the feminist and sexual revolutions.[1]

Lie #1: *You can have it all.*

Society would have women believe that they can be high-powered CEOs, devoted wives, loving mothers, impeccable dressers, immaculate homemakers, gourmet chefs, creative hostesses, and disciplined exercisers. And women in pursuit of this impossible goal pay the price of a sense of failure, lack of fulfillment, and utter exhaustion when they don't live up to those unreachable standards. After all, as Dr. Grant points out, women—like men—are only human!

At our seminars, though, Emilie and I are seeing more and more supermoms who have come to realize that they can't have it all and have decided that they don't even want to try. In growing numbers, women are leaving the hard-charging corporate world and returning to the responsibilities, challenges, and comforts of home, children, and family—and they are content with their choice. They tell us that they were paying too high a price in terms of their marriage, their children, their peace of mind, and their sanity when they were trying to achieve the illusory and impossible goals that society put before them.

Lie #2: *Men and women are fundamentally the same.*

This lie has caused many women to adopt attributes and behaviors that run counter to their natural characteristics and temperaments. These women have been untrue to themselves as they have tried to be other than what God created them to be.

Clinical studies show consistently different play patterns between young boys and girls, but we don't need sociologists and psychologists to point out the differences. Our own observations of the world around us and even limited contact with a member of the opposite sex reveal that men and women have different priorities, think different thoughts, and have different desires in life. The basic differences between males and females (which we'll address throughout this book) are one reason why marriage is challenging, and unfortunately, many women have refused to acknowledge these differences in their quest for liberation and equality with their male counterparts. Let me say here that *different* does not imply better or worse, superior or inferior. And, acknowledging that there are differences may help women be more comfortable being women—and not men!

Lie #3: *Desirability is enhanced by accomplishment.*

What makes a woman attractive to a man? Is it her keen business sense, her economic conquests in the corporate world, how many company boards she sits on, the number of postgraduate degrees she has earned, or the honors listed on her resumé? Does the power she attains by virtue of her many accomplishments win her the devotion of her man? Does love blossom where the woman has achieved much of what the world values in the way of status and success? No! Again, the world's lies have taken hold. This is not to say that women should not use their God-given gifts or strive to respond to God's call in their lives. Rather, women are learning that their accomplishments don't necessarily win them a man's attention or devotion. Women are also learning that the top of the corporate ladder can be as lonely for them as it is for men.

Lie #4: *Your full potential must be realized.*

God calls each of us to use the talents and abilities He has given us, but too many of us have fallen victim to the idea that we have incredible hidden potential and all of it must be realized. While it's true that we should do everything to the best of our ability, believing that we should always be able to win the gold medal or consistently score a perfect "10" can mean disappointment and depression when human limitations result in a bronze medal or an unexpected "8," "6," or even "2."

By contrast, the Bible offers a message of freedom. Again and again throughout the pages of Scripture, we see how God uses ordinary people in His work. We don't have to be mental giants, well-trained scholars, or experts in the Bible. We need only to surrender ourselves to God and allow Him to do great things through us. Jesus teaches, "Whoever exalts himself shall be humbled; and whoever humbles himself shall be exalted"

(Matthew 23:12). Resting on the truth of the Bible, we can be free from the myth of unrealized potential. Humbling ourselves before God yet willing to do our best wherever He calls us to work, we can let Him do what He will with our five loaves and two fish (Matthew 14:13-21).

Lie #5: *Men and women view sex in the same way.*

One basic difference between men and women is the way they approach and enjoy sex, and some of those differences are not hard to understand. First, the potential consequences of sexual intercourse—bearing a new life—have far greater ramifications in the life of a woman. In addition, the connection between sex and love is much closer and more important to women than it is to men, yet the sexual revolution has attempted to erase this difference. In their efforts to achieve equality with men, many sexually active women have tried to ignore their fundamental emotional needs. They have sacrificed their souls based on the lie that they should approach sex just as men do.

If women were to accept the fact that their Creator made them different from men, these women could again find wholeness, peace, and a more satisfying sexuality. Often women will ask, "How can I be more feminine?" My usual response is, "By being less masculine!" Men like the softness of a woman—her chin, her voice, her dress, her manners, her social graces, and the way she relates to them.

Lie #6: *Motherhood can be postponed without penalty.*

Quite often, women delay motherhood as they work toward their career goals. Some even postpone marriage for the sake of a career. In doing so, they ignore the fact that their reproductive system won't be able to reproduce forever. When they do suddenly hear the biological clock ticking, these women may panic. Their desperation for a child may then be heightened by any difficulty they have conceiving. Sadly, despite society's message to the contrary and today's high-tech medical advances, a woman's desire for children could end up never being fulfilled if she puts off motherhood too long.

Lie #7: *Today's woman should abandon "softness" for "assertiveness."*

The words *feminine* and *soft* no longer carry the positive associations they once did. Many women today are choosing assertiveness and strength—tools for the business world—over kindness, sensitivity, and compassion in their relationships. They don't seem to realize that attractiveness and real power come with the feminine characteristics given to them by God. We men respond to women who are vulnerable and open to our love and care. Today, too many women wrongly equate such vulnerability with weakness. As we've seen before in this list of lies, women lose when they try to be like men.

Lie #8: *Speaking one's mind is better than listening.*

With wisdom that contrasts sharply to this popular modern myth, the New Testament writer James instructs believers to "be quick to hear, slow to speak" (1:19). In our culture, however, which greatly values busyness, many of us—men and women alike—are more comfortable doing instead of being and speaking instead of listening. When women transfer their obsession for achievement from the corporate world to the arena of male–female relationships, they often fail to be the kind of listener that appeals to a man. Listening, which is a more passive and receptive role, has been granted second-class status. As a result, men and women alike miss out on the bond which compassionate listening can forge between them.

Lie #9: *A woman should be self-sufficient.*

Remember the feminist rallying cry, "A woman needs a man like a fish needs a bicycle"? This slogan points to the myth of self-sufficiency, a myth that led Dr. Grant to label the modern woman "the Amazon woman." In the legendary Amazon culture, women functioned completely apart from men. Once a year they would meet with men for breeding purposes, but then they returned to their own island to raise the children.

The attitude that women don't need men is in direct opposition to the plan of our Creator. Men and women are to honor one another and lift each other up, and we honor one another when we humble ourselves. The writer of Proverbs observed that "a man's pride will bring him low, but a humble spirit will obtain honor" (29:23). Jesus taught that "the greatest among you shall be your servant. And whoever exalts himself shall be humbled; and whoever humbles himself shall be exalted" (Matthew 23:11-12). The apostle Peter exhorted his readers to "humble yourselves, therefore, under the mighty hand of God, that He may exalt you at the proper time" (1 Peter 5:6). These teachings are quite contrary to our society's prescriptions about success and to the myth that women can exalt themselves above men as people they simply don't need.

A more humble and biblical attitude toward one's spouse enables a Christian marriage relationship to reflect—as it should—the relationship between Jesus and His church. Just as Christ "loved the church and gave Himself up for her" (Ephesians 5:25), husbands and wives are to humble themselves in service to one another. Furthermore, this godly marriage relationship

---

Me and Her

She is compulsive.
I am impulsive.
She likes it hot.
I like it cold.
She is neat.
I'm a slob.
Andy Rooney says, "A's marry Z's"
But we are in different alphabets.
I push.
She pulls.
She says, "Down."
I say, "Up.
She is night.
I am day.
Living together is hard.
Living without her would be impossible.

—Author unknown

---

is to be the foundation for raising children who will come to know, love, and serve the Lord. Many single parents today are doing their best to raise their children alone, but God's plan is to have husbands and wives be partners in this all-important and challenging task. The myth of feminine self-sufficiency sabotages God's design and runs counter to many biblical teachings.

Lie #10: *A woman should look for sensitivity, not strength, in a man.*

A softer, more sensitive man has not appealed to women the way people thought he would. While the new male sensitivity brings an important dimension to male–female relationships, women also want their men to be strong. So we men are left to figure out how to be strong without being obnoxiously macho, and sensitive without being weak. I hear many Christian men today wondering how to be both the man the Lord wants them to be and the man their wife or society wants them to be. Men today are desperately trying to figure out which characteristics are right and proper for them. When your husband manifests godly manhood, praise him. Help him become God's man.

Challenging the Lies

Consider again the litany of lies we've just looked at: Women can have it all, men and women are fundamentally the same, accomplishment means desirability, women must realize their full potential, men and women are alike in their attitudes and approach to sex, women can put off motherhood without penalty, women should be assertive instead of soft, speaking one's mind is better than listening, women don't need men, and women should look for sensitivity instead of strength in a man. Now consider the impact these lies have had on our society. What role have they played in the harsh realities of families breaking up and teenagers rebelling or being lost to drugs?

When we believe in and act on these lies, we not only undermine society, we also find ourselves living contrary to God's plan. When we try to change who God made men and women to be and redesign the plan He instituted in the beginning, our efforts dishonor the Creator. Despite that fact and despite the negative consequences of these lies, they still influence much of society's thinking about men and women. And speaking out against these lies and myths is not always well-received. Today everyone pressures us to be tolerant or "politically correct."

Remember when First Lady Barbara Bush addressed the women at Wellesley College? Her comments received harsh criticism from the all-women student body. Let's look again at what she said:

> At the end of your life, you will never regret not having passed one more test, not winning one more verdict, or not closing one more deal. You will regret time not spent with a husband, a child, a friend, or a parent.
>
> We are in a transitional period right now—fascinating and exhilarating times, learning to adjust to changes and the choices we—men and women—are facing. As an example, I remember what a friend said on hearing her husband complain to his buddies that he had to babysit: Quickly setting him straight, my friend told her husband that when it's your own kids, it's not called babysitting.
>
> Now, maybe we should adjust faster and maybe we should adjust slower. But whatever the era, whatever the times, one thing will never change: Fathers and mothers, if you have children, they must come first. You must read to your children, and you must hug your children, and you must love your children. Your success as a family, our success as a society depends not on what happens in the White House but on what happens inside your house.[2]

Barbara Bush boldly spoke out against some of the lies women and men alike have fallen prey to. In doing so, she challenged women of all ages across America to evaluate the choices they are making and the impact those choices are having on American society. In effect, Mrs. Bush called women to deny the lies society has propagated over the past few decades.

And the teachings of the Bible—as we'll see in this book—call women to do likewise. Will you respond to the call?

Keeping Your Commitment

On Mother's Day 1991, our local newspaper ran a story that speaks to our times. Letha Blacman recalled the day when, pregnant with her first child, she left her husband of two years and went home to her mother. When she arrived, she spent 30 minutes telling her mother what she was unhappy about and that she was leaving her husband and their home. (Interestingly, at the time the article was written, Letha couldn't remember why she was so angry with her husband!)

When Letha stopped talking, her mother said, "I have listened to you, and now I am going to tell you what you are going to do. You are expecting a child. It needs a mother and a father. You are going back to your husband, and the two of you are going to raise that child."

I can do everything God asks me to with the help of Christ who gives me the strength and power.

—Philippians 4:13 TLB

The next morning, Letha's husband went to her mother's house and took Letha home. Angry that her mother hadn't opened her arms and said, "Come home, honey," Letha didn't even wave goodbye as she and her husband drove away.

Love in Action

- Accept your husband's suggestions without negative body language.
- Call him at work to tell him you love him.
- Do what you tell him you are going to do.
- Let him choose his favorite radio station in the house or in the car.
- Bring him his favorite refresher drink when he is working on a project.

The punch line of the story? Letha and her husband raised that first child and a second as well. On April 23, 1991, they celebrated their fifty-ninth wedding anniversary.[3] Letha had decided to stand by her commitment when she felt like quitting. Today's society would have told her to be concerned about her own happiness and encouraged her to make it on her own. But fortunately she took a stand, and you can do the same.

You can support your man when you feel like quitting. You can stay at his side even when circumstances are tough and the struggle is intense. With guidance from Scripture and reliance on God's strength, you can survive the difficult times and do so with patience, love, and hope.

May you know the sparkle
as this day unfolds
of precious dewdrops a
violet holds;
May you see the colors of
spectrums above;
May you know the blessing
of friends and God's love.

—June Masters Bacher

2

Knowing the Hope God Offers

By wisdom a house is built, and by understanding it is established; and by knowledge the rooms are filled with all precious and pleasant riches.

—Proverbs 24:3,4

Whenever I buy a new insurance policy, household appliance, or pair of jeans, I pay attention to the disclaimers:

- "It is agreed that no insurance shall be effective unless the applicant passes a complete medical examination."
- "This warranty is valid only if the product is used for the purpose for which it was designed. It does not cover products which have been damaged by negligence, misuse, or accident or which have been modified or repaired by unauthorized persons."
- "Wash and dry with like colors. Color may transfer when new. Wash before wearing. Shrinks approximately 10%."

We consumers live in a world of disclaimers. Manufacturers regularly provide guidelines for the use and care of their products and give specifics about when they will (or won't) stand behind their work. Their instructions also keep consumers from having expectations that exceed what the item can deliver.

Being Realistic

Before we get too far along in this book, I also want to put forth several disclaimers. Like today's manufacturers, I don't want you to expect more than what this book can deliver, so I offer the following five points.

1. *Simple, surefire formulas don't exist.*

I would love to be able to give you a little white pill that would ease all your concerns and answer all your questions, but there aren't any such pills on the market. It would be nice to be able to find an easy, clearly marked path out of the many difficulties we face, but not even in Scripture do we find that life is going to be easy or that we can avoid having to cope with life's challenges.

Perhaps you're looking for the answers to questions like these:

- How can I have a good marriage?
- How can I be the kind of wife my husband wants to live with?
- How can I help my husband stop drinking?
- How can I keep my children drug-free?

There are no instant formulas for dealing with issues like these. Also, what works for one person or situation won't necessarily work for another.

Although God's Word doesn't offer us pat formulas for living, it *does* offer us guidelines for living a meaningful Christian life, building a solid Christian marriage, and raising children who know and love the Lord. In the chapters that follow, we'll look at these guidelines and trust God to show you how to apply them to your specific circumstances. Again, there are no guarantees that your life will be free of pain, heartache, and disappointment, but you can find hope in God's love for you and the promise that He "causes all things to work together for good to those who love God" (Romans 8:28).

2. *Wives are not to be change agents.*

Many people who say "I do" think that after they are married their spouses will change. But nowhere in Scripture does God appoint spouses to be change agents for one another.

Despite that fact, many women I meet at our seminars ask me how they can change their husbands. I gently remind them that the Holy Spirit—not the wife—is the change agent. Speaking on this same issue, Ruth Graham wisely says, "Tell your mate the positive, and tell God the negative." Talk to God about your marriage. Ask your heavenly Father to work change through His Spirit—and be aware that He may change you as well as your spouse! Also, focus your efforts on the role that Scripture clearly sets forth for you: "Be subject to one another in the fear of Christ. Wives, be subject to your own husbands, as to the Lord. . . . And let the wife see to it that she respect her husband" (Ephesians 5:21,22,33). Women are not to seek to change their husbands. Rather, they are called to honor their husbands out of honor for the Lord. (Likewise, men are not to seek to change their wives, and I know from experience what results from such efforts. Whenever I've tried to change Emilie, I've provoked tension, discouragement, and resistance in her.

Consider the fact that, as fallen human beings, we have a strong tendency to do the opposite of what we are told to do. We want to touch wet paint when the sign says "Wet Paint." Children want to test the "no" when we instruct them to stay away from matches, water, and friends we don't approve of. Likewise, our spouses may end up doing the opposite of what we suggest when, usually through negative communications, we try to change them. Discouraged—if not angered—by our criticism, our spouses can come to resent our words and inwardly resolve, "I'll show him/her!" In such situations, we can actually hamper God's work in the lives of our mates. God, working through His Spirit, is to be the change agent. We can end up hindering His work in the lives of our spouses when we try to be helpful with criticism that is anything but constructive.

Through the years, God has also shown me that many times my *responses* to Emilie's shortcomings were worse than the shortcomings themselves! I have found myself, for instance, becoming angry, unkind, resentful, and moody in the face of her shortcomings, and these responses impeded our relationship and my walk with the Lord. Even today I remember how negative I became when I tried to change her—but I honestly can't remember the specific shortcoming I was trying to correct! I do remember, though, coming across the exhortation of Ephesians 4:29: "Let no unwholesome word proceed from your mouth, but only such a word as is good for edification according to the need of the moment, that it may give grace to those who hear." That verse led me to adopt "Is that edifying?" as a guideline for my speech, and that little question has really helped me make sure all my words to Emilie are positive.

Experience has also taught me that husbands and wives alike need to be sensitive to verbal and nonverbal messages we send to our spouses, and we need to ask forgiveness for any improper responses we might make. Rather than making insensitive and inappropriate efforts to change our mates, we must support them in prayer and be willing to wait for the Holy Spirit to do His work in their lives.

When it comes to seeing changes in a spouse, many women (and men) don't want to wait, and often self-centeredness is the main reason. Wives want their men to fit their ideals for the perfect husband—now! Are you one of those wives? Consider your attitude toward your husband in light of this instruction from Scripture:

> Do nothing from selfishness or empty conceit, but with humility of mind let each of you regard one another as more important than himself; do not merely look out

for your own personal interests, but also for the interests of others (Philippians 2:3,4).

We are to be subject to our mate out of fear (or reverence) for God, and we are to ask God to help us love our mates as He calls us to.

Instead of focusing on changing your mate, concentrate on what God wants from you. First Peter 3:1,2 lets women know how to live with an unresponsive mate: "Wives, fit in with your husbands' plans; for then if they refuse to listen when you talk to them about the Lord, they will be won by your respectful, pure behavior. Your godly lives will speak to them better than any words" (TLB). Is this easy to do? Not until you accept the fact that God designed marriage relationships to work best according to His guidelines.

When both the husband and wife are submitting to Jesus as their Lord and Savior, both will be living according to God's plans for marriage, and both will be open to the work of the Holy Spirit in their lives as individuals and in their life together. And again, the Holy Spirit is the one who changes our spouses—and changes us—to conform to the image of Christ. In light of that fact, this book is more a "how to love and pray for your spouse" than a "how to change your spouse" manual.

3. *Each of us carries baggage from childhood.*

Today, the word *baggage* is used to describe more than the suitcases we carry when we travel. Today the word also refers to the behaviors, thought patterns, and deep-seated wounds we carry. This baggage weighs us down and keeps us from being the people God wants us to be. Not surprisingly, this often-hidden baggage also interferes with our relationships, keeps wives from knowing

Remember, ladies, you are married to a sinner, and so is he.

—ELISABETH ELLIOT

their husbands, and causes painful and frustrating conflicts in a marriage.

This book cannot free you from that baggage or heal the hurts from your past experiences. It can, however, remind you that your husband—like you—entered the relationship with some kind of baggage. It can also call you to confess any current baggage—the sin that prevents you from being all that God wants you to be. Freeing yourself from baggage—both past and present—will enable you to be an encourager to your man.

4. *We are at war with the enemy.*

Paul wrote in Ephesians 6, "Our struggle is not against flesh and blood, but against the rulers, against the powers, against the world forces of this darkness, against the spiritual forces of wickedness in the heavenly places" (verse 12). We believers truly are at war with Satan and his army, and he would love to destroy our marriages. After all, good marriages are a testimony to God and His love. God wants us to have healthy relationships based in Him, but Satan wishes to confuse our lives so that we no longer know what is right. Your daily newspaper with its stories of murder, hatred, runaways, divorce, and death shows that Satan is alive and well and hard at work causing confusion and heartache in our world.

As part of his work, Satan the deceiver may send a coworker, unsaved friend, or neighbor with advice for one of your problems. Weigh that advice to see if it meets the standards of Scripture. If the advice contradicts or undermines God's Word, then you won't want to follow it.

Keep in mind, too, that Satan can bring struggles and difficulty to your marriage, and the solution he will whisper into you ear is, "Run!" This book can't protect you from the battle with Satan, but it can remind you that the Holy Spirit says, "Stay," and that the Spirit will help you do just that (Ephesians 6:10-17). When you pray to the Lord about your struggles, you may find it helpful to pray using Scripture. For example, you could say, "I pray that You, the eternal God, would be my husband's refuge and that you would drive out the enemy from before him" (see Deuteronomy 33:27).

5. *We are all sinners.*

In Romans 3:23, the apostle Paul teaches that "all have sinned and fall short of the glory of God." As sinners, we are not perfect; all of us—wives as well as husbands—fall short of God's commands and our spouse's expectations. When your husband disappoints you, don't be surprised. Even though he is a believer who has been cleansed from his sin, he brings into your marriage—as you do—the human propensity to sin. At times we succumb to the desires of the flesh, and we do things contrary to what we would like to do (Romans 7:15). We end up hurting the very people we love. This book can't keep you or your husband from giving in to sin. But it can and will call you to follow in the footsteps of Jesus and extend to your husband forgiveness, patience, and unconditional love.

Finding Hope in God's Grace

After reading about all that this book can't deliver, you may be wondering, *Where, then, can I find hope?* Perhaps you've felt hopeless about some of the circumstances in your life, family, or marriage. Well, one thing this book *can* do is help replace that hopelessness with the hope of God that never disappoints.

As Dr. Larry Crabb reminds his readers in his book *The Marriage Builder*, the hope of the Christian lies not in a change of circumstances that God may or may not bring about, but in the grace of God. We aren't to hope that our spouse will change, our business will turn around, or our children will straighten out. Instead, we are to hope in God's grace—in His unearned, undeserved, and unconditional love for us.

Larry Crabb writes:

> Remember that the Lord has not promised to put your marriage together for you. The hope of the Christian is not that one's spouse will change or that

> one's health will improve or that one's financial situation will become good. God does not promise to rearrange our worlds to suit our longings. He does promise to permit only those events that will further His purpose in our lives. Our responsibility is to respond to life's events in a manner intended to please the Lord, not to change our spouses into what we want. . . . Certainly if both partners build on the foundation of hope and strive earnestly to live biblically, even the worst marriage can be turned around. Either way, there is a reason to hope. This reason is bound up in the truth of the grace of God.[4]

This call to rest in God's grace is one of the most important messages for the Christian church today. We need to realize that anything and everything we are going through in our marriage is the forge God is using to work in *our own* life, not the life of our mate. God is dealing with you and your relationship to Jesus Christ, and how you honor that relationship within your marriage is to be your primary concern. As you focus on becoming the person God wants you to be, you will see and experience His grace in your life, and that grace will mean hope and perhaps even change in your marriage.

Take a moment right now to ask God what He is trying to teach you. Ask Him to show you what He is doing so that you can better understand and accept the challenges you are facing. You might not receive an immediate answer, but taking a moment to seek refuge in God through prayer will give you a taste of the hope and the peace God can give to you. Think back, too, on past times when you struggled to know what God was doing in your life. Looking back, do you see now how God was at work? Let those incidents be touchstones of faith that will encourage you to persevere today.

Removing Some Stumbling Blocks

I also encourage you to reevaluate your expectations for your marriage. It's common for women to enter marriage with unrealistic or, at best, clouded expectations that came from childhood dreams, popular novels, movies, and television programs, and these expectations often result in what Dennis and Barbara Rainey call "the phantom husband":

> He rises early, has a quiet time reading the Bible and praying, and then jogs several seven-minute miles. After breakfast with his family, he presents a fifteen-minute devotional. Never forgetting to hug and kiss his wife good-bye, he arrives at work ten minutes early. He is consistently patient with his co-workers, always content with his job, and has problem-solving techniques for every situation. At lunch he eats only perfectly healthy foods. His desk is never cluttered, and he is confidently in control. He arrives home on time every day and never turns down his boys when they want to play catch.
>
> This phantom is well-read in world events, politics, key issues of our day, the Scriptures, and literary classics. He's a handyman around the house and loves to build things for his wife. He is socially popular and never tires of people or of helping them in time of need. He obeys all traffic laws and never speeds, even if he's late. He can quote large sections of Scripture in a single bound, has faith more powerful than a locomotive, and is faster than a speeding bullet in solving family conflicts. He never gets discouraged, never wants to quit, and always has the right words for every circumstance. He also keeps his garage neat. He never loses things, always flosses his teeth, and has no trouble with his weight. And he has time to fish.[5]

While the Raineys' words may have made you smile, they may also have opened your eyes to some of the unrealistic and unfair expectations women can have for their husbands. Although the world would lead women to believe that they can have it all in the way of the perfect career, a perfect home, perfect children, and the perfect husband, the Bible teaches otherwise. Jesus teaches that we will have trouble in this world—yet He also says that He has overcome the world (John 16:33). So don't let false expectations—that ideal and purely imaginary phantom husband—keep you from learning all that

God wants to teach you and experiencing all that God has for you in your marriage.

Consider, too, the wisdom of the Hawaiians. A few years ago after doing a seminar in Honolulu, Emilie and I were taking a bus to the airport on a rainy Sunday morning. Commenting on the rain, the driver stated, "Today will be a celebration for some newlyweds." Looking out the window, I saw nothing but rain and couldn't understand why the driver said that. I asked her, "What do you mean it will be a celebration?" She replied, "In Hawaii, we say that rain on your wedding day is cause to celebrate." I thought to myself, *In California, rain on a wedding day wouldn't be a cause for celebration—it would be a disaster.* We want and even demand perfection. Our Hawaiian counterparts, though, have learned to live with imperfection. Have you learned to do the same in your marriage?

Living with a Purpose

Imperfection in the world—in our home, our spouse, and ourself—is easier to live with when we are reaching for something greater than anything this world can offer. What are you reaching for? What is your purpose in life? Have you selected a Scripture verse that helps you to clarify or express your purpose in life? If you haven't thought about this, why not do so now? God's living Word does indeed have truth, guidance, and hope for you. Find a verse that will bring those to you, and let it serve as a purpose statement for your life.

Emilie and I have chosen Matthew 6:33 as our theme verse: "Seek first His kingdom and His righteousness; and all these things shall be added to you." In all our decisions, Emilie and I ask the basic question, "Are we seeking first God's kingdom and His righteousness?" Through the years, this verse has given us direction and purpose.

Say no to the good things in life and save your yeses for the best.

In Emilie's book *Survival for Busy Women* and our coauthored work *The 15 Minute Money Manager*, we explain how you can develop long- and short-range goals that are based on your purpose statement and that will help you meet that purpose. When you have set forth specific goals that will help you fulfill your purpose in life, you can more easily determine your priorities. If certain activities or opportunities don't help you reach your goals for your life in general and your marriage in particular, you may want to say, "No, thank you."

Living life with a purpose can change despair to hope, and hope will give you joy even when life is difficult. Living with a purpose rooted in God's truth will also help you experience more fully the grace of God that saved you and can make you unselfish, humble, kind, considerate, patient, wise, and loving to your marriage partner as well as to others.

Surviving the "Tunnel of Chaos"

Do you find yourself wanting to experience the hope of God's grace, remove from your marriage unrealistic expectations and demands for perfection, and live with a purpose that is more important than the irritations of day-to-day life, yet feel as if getting there seems too risky?

Author and pastor Bill Hybels shares with his readers some ideas about moving toward open, honest, and authentic relationships. Bill explains that the call to truth and authenticity must have greater value than simply maintaining peace in the relationship. This call to truth challenges us to address and resolve misunderstandings, share feelings, talk through offenses, and deal with doubts about each other's integrity. Hybels calls this experience "the tunnel of chaos." This tunnel is where "hurts are unburied,

> *Serenity depends on a certain mental attitude—an attitude which accepts. We have to train ourselves to appreciate the good gifts of God, material, mental and spiritual. Among all God's gifts there is none greater than Christ himself.*
>
> —Gordon Powell

hostilities revealed, and tough questions asked." When misunderstandings are not resolved, relationships deteriorate. In Hybels' words, "The secret agendas of hurt and misunderstanding lead to detachment, distrust, and bitterness. Feelings of love begin to die. It's the story of too many marriages, family relationships, and friendships. . . . No matter how unpleasant the tunnel of chaos is, there's no other route to authentic relationships.[6]

When we truly want the peace that awaits on the other side of the tunnel and are willing to deal with the chaos in the tunnel, then we are ready to move ahead. The risks are real and the work is difficult, but the rewards of an authentic relationship are worth the treacherous journey. Inside the tunnel, explosions happen, rocks fall, lights go out, horns blow, and people shout—but what a beautiful sunlit morning awaits on the other side.

Are you standing at the mouth of the tunnel today, wanting what is on the other side but afraid to enter? Recall for a moment your wedding vows, those promises you made to your husband and to God. Being true to those vows will cost you (it costs everyone), but God's rewards for such obedience will be a great blessing. The tunnel may appear dark and confusing, and the battles that await you may seem overwhelming, but I encourage you to take that first step. After all, how do you move a mountain? You pick up and move the first stone. Then the next. And the next.

How do you survive the tunnel of chaos? A step at a time . . . and that will get you to the other side.

Expressions of Love

- Listen to his dreams.
- Read a book aloud to each other.
- Give him a certificate for a foot rub.
- Ask him what his favorite meal is and prepare it for him soon.
- Give him time to unwind when he comes home from work.

3

Standing by God

I love the Lord because he hears my prayers and answers them. Because he bends down and listens, I will pray as long as I breathe!

—Psalm 116:1,2 TLB

Perhaps you're surprised by the title of this chapter. Do you wonder what standing by God has to do with supporting your man? Let me assure you that the connection is vital. Nurturing your relationship with the Lord is crucial to being the kind of woman and wife He calls you to be.

Consider the fruit that comes from spending time with your heavenly Father. In Galatians 5, Paul writes that "the fruit of the Spirit is love, joy, peace, patience, kindness, goodness, faithfulness, gentleness, self-control" (verses 22,23). Think about each item in that list. How will each of those God-given qualities enable you to stand by your man? Which of us doesn't need a touch of God's love, joy, peace, patience, kindness, goodness, faithfulness, gentleness, and self-control in our marriage? Those are the things—as well as guidance, wisdom, hope, and a deeper knowledge of Him—that He wants to give to us, His children.

FINDING TIME OR MAKING TIME?

"But," you say, "who has time? My 'to do' list is always longer than my day. I run from the time the alarm goes off every morning until I fall into bed at night. How can I possibly find time to do one more thing? When can I find even a few minutes to read the Bible or pray?"

Allow me to answer your questions with a question: Are you doing what's important during your day, or only what is urgent? Your relationship with Jesus Christ is the most important part of your life. Isn't that what the Bible tells us?

Let me also share a saying that is important to Emilie and me: "People do what they want to do." All of us make choices, and when we don't make time for God in our day, we are probably not making the best choices.

I'm going to heaven and I believe I'm going by the blood of Christ. That's not popular preaching but I'll tell you it's all the way through the Bible and I may be the last fellow on earth who preaches it, but I'm going to preach it because it's the only way we're going to get there.

—BILLY GRAHAM

God greatly desires to spend time alone with you. After all, you are His child (John 1:12; Galatians 3:26). He created you, He loves you, and He gave His only Son for your salvation. Your heavenly Father wants to know you, and He wants you to know Him. The Creator of the universe wants to meet with you alone daily, and that daily communion with Him is indeed the best way to get to know Him. How can you and I say no to that opportunity?

MEETING WITH GOD

So how can you get to know your heavenly Father? Simply by spending time alone with Him. It doesn't matter what time you meet with Him, or where you spend that time. The only requirement for a rich time with God is to have a willing heart.

Your meeting time with God is likely to vary according to the schedule you have at any given time. Even Jesus' prayer times varied. He often slipped away to be alone in prayer (Luke 5:16). He prayed in the morning (Mark 1:35) and late at night (Matthew 14:23), on a hill (Luke 22:41-45) and in the Upper Room (John 17). In Southern California, where commute times can be long, I know people who use their driving time to be with God. When our children were still at home, Emilie used to get up earlier than the rest of the family for a quiet time of reading Scripture and praying.

Much of my time studying and preparing to teach a lesson serves as my quiet time with the Lord. Even when I don't have a lesson to prepare, I take time to read God's Word and dwell upon His thoughts. And I love it when we get to church early and I have 10 or 15 minutes to read my Bible and think upon God's wisdom and provision. Amid the distracting talk that is often going on around me, I use this block of time to set my heart and prepare to worship. (In fact, I believe if others in the congregation devoted this time to reading Scripture and praying for the service, they would be more responsive to the pastor's messages and church would be more meaningful for every worshiper.)

Again, the times and places where we meet God will vary, but the fact that we meet alone with God each day should be a constant in our lives. After all, God has made it clear that He is interested in and cares for all who are His children, including you and me (1 Peter 5:7).

Getting Started

Perhaps you want to spend time with God each day but aren't sure where to start. Open with a word of greeting. In a short prayer, ask God's blessing on your time together. One small group I belonged to would open the morning meetings with a song, and you may want to greet God with a song, too. Don't worry if you don't have a good voice. God cares more about your heart!

Reading God's Word

After you greet the Lord, spend some time reading the Bible. Jesus teaches that we can't live by bread alone; we need God's Word to nourish and sustain us (Matthew 4:4). If you're not sure where to begin, I recommend starting with the Gospel of John. If you're getting acquainted with the Bible for the first time, it's in the book of John that you'll find God's love for you beautifully explained and His plan for you carefully outlined.

As you read the Bible, think about the words and meditate on them. To *meditate* simply means to think seriously about spiritual things. Think quietly, soberly, and deeply about God—about how wonderful He is, what blessings He has given you, and what He wants you to do. As you read and meditate, you may notice one or more of the following:

- A special promise you can claim
- A principle to help you in your daily life
- A command you should follow
- A light that reveals some sin in your life
- A meaningful verse that you'll want to memorize
- Comfort or insight for the hard times you're facing
- Guidance for the day ahead
- Hope that encourages you and that you can share with someone you care about

Don't read too quickly or try to cover too much material in one sitting. Take the time to look for all that God has specifically for you in the verses you read.

Spending Time in Prayer

After you've read and meditated on God's Word for awhile, spend some time with God in prayer. Talk to Him as you would to one of your parents or a special friend who loves you, desires the best for you, and wants to help you in every way possible.

Are you wondering what to talk to God about when you pray? Here are a few suggestions:

- Praise God for who He is: the Creator and Sustainer of the whole universe, who is interested in each of us who are in His family (Psalm 150; Luke 12:6,7).
- Thank God for all He has done for you . . . for all He is doing for you . . . and for all that He will do for you in the future (Philippians 4:6).
- Confess your sins. Tell God about the things you have done and said and thought for which you are sorry. He tells us in 1 John 1:9 that He is "faithful and righteous to forgive us our sins."
- Pray for your family . . . and for friends or neighbors who have needs, physical or spiritual. Ask God to work in the heart of someone you hope will come to know Jesus as Savior.
- Pray for our government officials, for your minister and church officers, for missionaries and other Christian servants (Philippians 2:4; 1 Timothy 2:1,2).
- Pray, too, for yourself. Ask for guidance for the day ahead. Ask God to help you do His will . . . and ask Him to arrange opportunities to serve Him throughout the day (Philippians 4:6). Know that time spent with your heavenly Father is never wasted. If you spend time alone with God in the morning, you'll start your day refreshed and ready for whatever comes your way. If you spend time alone with Him in the evening, you'll go to sleep relaxed, resting in His care and ready for a new day to serve Him.

Remember, too, that you can talk to Him anytime and anywhere—in school, at work, on the freeway, at home—about anything. You don't have to make an appointment to ask Him for something you need or to thank Him for something you have received from Him. God is interested in everything that happens to you at all times.

Developing a Prayer Notebook

In Colossians 4:2, the apostle Paul gives us this encouragement: "Devote yourselves to prayer, keeping alert in it with an attitude of thanksgiving."

Like any other activity, your prayers will be more consistent when you approach your prayers in an organized way and you are aware of God's answers to your prayers. In our More Hours in Your Day seminar, we suggest how you can easily manage this very important facet of your life by developing your own prayer notebook. All you need is a three-ring binder (we recommend 9″x 5″), a set of tabs, and 100 sheets of lined paper that fit into your binder. In your notebook, you'll want to keep track of prayer requests and have space for sermon outlines, notes, and any special verses or messages you want to apply to your life. (See page 50 for sample.)

1. First, label six of the tabs with the days "Monday" through "Saturday" and insert several pieces of paper behind each divider.
2. Then label one tab "Sunday." This is where you'll place your sermon notes (see page 51 for a sample format you can use).
3. Use two more tabs for miscellaneous sections. These sections might include Bible study notes (see page 52 for sample), a record of your daily Bible readings, personal prayers, favorite Scriptures, a list of Scriptures you've memorized, personal goals, and even names, addresses, and phone numbers.
4. Now, on a separate piece of paper, make a list of prayer requests. You can use the following headings:
   - Family (immediate and extended)
   - Personal (your relationship with God, your role as homemaker, your weaknesses, your relationships with people, your goals, and so on)
   - Finances (budgetary concerns, decisions about major purchases, investments, saving for retirement, home improvements)
   - Illness (Great Grandma Gertie's hip, Aunt Barbara's lupus, your special friend's addiction, Bill's glaucoma, and so on)

- Career (challenges, decisions, needs)
- Government/Schools (the president of the United States, state and city leaders, day-care centers, colleges, your local school board, your children's teachers)
- Church (your pastor, the staff, the youth, and others who serve in your church)
- Missions (ministries and missions like Campus Crusade for Christ, Focus on the Family, Billy Graham, InterVarsity, Bible Study Fellowship, "More Hours in My Day," Navigators, Wycliffe Bible Translators, Young Life, Youth for Christ, the 700 Club, missionaries you know or know of).

5. Now decide which topics you'll pray about on which day of the week. Leave your weekly day of worship for your sermon notes. Your week may look like this:

   Monday—family (use one page for each member)
   Tuesday—church and missions
   Wednesday—personal
   Thursday—finances and career
   Friday—illness
   Saturday or Sunday—government/schools

   (At the top of each page, place a picture of the person or people for whom you are praying. That may prove helpful for your time of prayer. Most people will gladly provide you with a picture if they know you are praying for them.)

Your prayer notebook will help you organize your concerns, watch for God's answers to your prayers, and note the words of encouragement and hope that God reveals to you in His Word. When Emilie hears of prayer needs, she first records them on her list of "Prayer Requests." Later she transfers them to the appropriate page in her notebook and prays for that item at the same time she prays for similar concerns. For example, she will pray for Bevan's fever on Friday as she prays for other people who are fighting illnesses.

> We are in too big a hurry, and we run by far more than we catch up with. The Bible tells us to "be still, and know that I am God" (PSALM 46:10 KJV). Beauty doesn't shout. Loveliness is quiet. Our finest moods are not clamorous. The familiar appeals of the Divine are always in calm tones—a still, small voice.
>
> —CHARLES L. ALLEN

As you keep track of what you want to pray for, your prayer life will be more satisfying than any hit-or-miss approach you may have used before. And, as you keep a record of your prayer requests and God's answers, you'll find your prayer life more rewarding. Keeping a prayer notebook, then, can greatly enrich your Christian walk.

Making a Prayer Basket

Even with a prayer notebook, Emilie soon realized that she could easily be discouraged about keeping her prayer time if she had to run around the house to get her Bible, a pencil, and her notebook. So she decided to make a "prayer basket." In it, she places all of her tools for her appointment with God:

- Her prayer notebook
- A pencil or pen
- Her Bible
- Some tissue for when tears come
- A small bouquet of fresh or silk flowers to remind her of God's love and of His Spirit
- A few cheery note cards for writing a note of encouragement to a friend or relative

If you have a prayer basket like Emilie's, you'll always be ready for your special time with Jesus.

You may also find it helpful to set aside a special spot to meet with the Lord. Depending on the time of year, you could sit by your fireplace with a cup of hot tea, or go outside under a tree with a glass of iced tea. Find a spot free of distractions and away from interruptions. Maybe you have a favorite chair that you can use only for this time with the Lord. That way, you'll know that when you sit down in that chair, you are there to meet with God.

One more word about your prayer basket: Besides keeping you organized, it will serve as a concrete reminder of the time you want to spend alone with the Lord. If you haven't picked up your basket in a day or two, that little straw friend of yours will cry out when you pass by and say, "Pick me up so we can spend time with Jesus!"

Learning from Model Prayers

As we spend time with God, we open ourselves to His work in our hearts and lives. Then, as we see Him working, we will want to know Him even more. We will want our prayer life to be all that it can be. Do you want that for your prayer life? Let's find out how that is possible.

In Scripture, we find many models of prayer, and probably foremost among those prayers is the Lord's Prayer (Matthew 6:9-13). This wonderful example includes important elements that we can include in our prayers: words of adoration, of submission to God's will for our life, of petition, and, in closing, of praise. We can learn much from the model our Lord gave when His disciples said, "Teach us to pray" (Luke 11:1).

I have also found Colossians 1:9-12 to be a powerful guide in my prayer life. If you aren't in the habit of praying or if you want to renew your time with God, I challenge you to read this passage of Scripture every day for 30 days. Look at it in small pieces, dwell on its message each day, take action upon what it says, and you'll become a new person.

Read how Paul and Timothy prayed for the church at Colossae:

> We . . . ask that you may be filled with the knowledge of His will in all spiritual wisdom and understanding, so that you may walk in a manner worthy of the Lord, to please Him in all respects, bearing fruit in every good work and increasing in the knowledge of God; strengthened with all power, according to His glorious might, for the attaining of all steadfastness and patience; joyously giving thanks to the Father, who has qualified us to share in the inheritance of the saints in light.

Now read the prayer again and think about what a wonderful prayer it is for you to pray for your husband and children. I know for a fact that Emilie has prayed for me every day of our marriage, and I am sorry I cannot say that I have done the same for her. Knowing that Emilie is praying for me is a real source of encouragement and support. If you aren't praying for your husband daily, let me suggest that Colossians 1:9-12 be your model. Look at what requests you'll be placing before God:

- That your husband will have the spiritual wisdom and understanding he needs to know God's will (verse 9).
- That your husband will "walk in a manner worthy of the Lord, to please Him in all respects" (verse 10).
- That your husband will bear "fruit in every good work and increase in the knowledge of God" (verse 10).
- That your husband will be "strengthened with all power . . . for the attaining of all steadfastness and patience" (verse 11).
- You would then end your prayer by joyously giving thanks to God for all that He has given you—your husband being one of those gifts (verse 12).

What armor of protection and growth you can give your husband with a prayer like that! With the Lord's provision in these ways, your husband will be able to deal with the challenges he faces.

I encourage you to tell your husband that you are praying for him every day. If he is receptive, tell him the specifics of your prayers for him. Let me assure you that it is a real comfort to know my wife is asking God to give me wisdom and understanding, enable me to honor Him in all I do, help me bear fruit for His kingdom, and grant me strength, steadfastness, and patience.

Know, too, that these verses from Colossians can also serve as a good model for your prayers for other family members, your Christian friends and neighbors, and yourself. After all, everyone who is a child of God needs to know His will; honor Him in everything; grow in the knowledge of the Lord; and be strong, steadfast, and patient.

Keeping a Journal

As you write out your daily prayers, you'll become more aware of how you feel about yourself, your husband, your children, and the circumstances of your life. You will become aware of the thoughts that are running through your mind. Keeping track of these feelings and thoughts in a journal can be an excellent means of growing spiritually and personally.

Emilie also encourages women to keep a daily journal when they go through a traumatic event in their life, and many have written to say how much they appreciated the idea. How many times have you thought, *I won't forget that thought/event/feeling*, and later wished you had written it down? If you keep a journal—during the smooth times as well as the rough—you will be able to look back at past events and recall them as if they had happened yesterday.

So You Want More?

When becoming a godly woman is a priority and you are faithfully spending time alone with your heavenly Father, you will see him blessing you with the fruit of the Spirit. He will fill your life more and more with "love, joy, peace, patience, kindness, goodness, faithfulness, gentleness, self-control" (Galatians 5:22,23). Your husband will notice these qualities, and so will your children. Is that what you'd like to see happen in your life? Here are some suggestions:

Focus on Jesus Christ. From the time you wake up to the time you fall asleep, try to be aware of Jesus' presence with you. Emilie and I start each day with a word of inspiration taken from a devotional book or easel-type flip charts that we have. Among our favorite devotionals are Oswald Chambers's *My Utmost for His Highest*, H. Norman Wright's *Quiet Time for Couples*, and Charles H. Spurgeon's *Morning and Evening.* We then try to carry that word with us throughout the day to remind us of a certain truth about or promise from Him. When you find a passage that is especially meaningful, don't be afraid to underline it, mark it with a highlighter pen, or make notes in the book margin. Books that are marked up will, in time, become good friends that remind you of what you learned in your walk with God.

Study God's Word daily. When you start the day with a devotional reading, you might come across a specific point or key verse that you'd like to study in greater depth. A chain-reference Bible is an excellent tool for this purpose. The Thompson Chain Reference Bible, for instance, is available in the King James and the New International Versions, and it

Expressions of Love

- Write your husband a thank-you card for just being himself. Place it on or under his pillow.
- Make his favorite dinner on Sunday evening.
- After his evening bath or shower give him a shoulder rub.
- Keep asking him what his dreams and visions are, and remember to affirm them.
- Go through his sock drawer and neaten it. Toss out the faded and worn socks.

has an excellent assortment of Bible study helps, including an index and a reasonably complete concordance.

For your Bible study times, consider using a Bible with cross-references and margin notes as well as footnotes. These extra features can direct you to other passages that are similar in content or thought. Talk to the staff at your local Christian bookstore; they can help you choose the Bible that will serve you best.

When you read and study your Bible, use your highlighter pen liberally. (Be sure to get the kind made especially for Bibles so the ink doesn't bleed through the thin paper.) Also, take time to write your thoughts in the margins. You might, as I do, date a passage of Scripture when it has particular relevance to the circumstances of your life or the topic which you are studying. Make note of new understandings you gain from familiar verses. When you do these things, the Bible becomes a much more personal guide and friend.

Should you decide to supplement your Bible reading with a devotional or a study guide, take some time to check the many different types of devotionals and study guides that are available. Again, the staff at your local Christian bookstore can recommend appropriate resources for you.

Let me also encourage you to get involved in a Bible Study Fellowship group if there is one in your area. This international organization sponsors community Bible studies for women (and men, but in separate groups), and is known for its very competent leaders and excellent materials.

Write out your prayers. Well-known authors Fred and Florence Littauer encourage their readers to spend 30 minutes or so in prayer after their time of daily Bible study. At first, Fred wondered how we would fill that much time in prayer, but now he rarely prays for less than half an hour.

What caused the change? Writing out his prayers word for word. Every day he opens his prayer notebook and writes until he's finished praying. He dates each entry and indicates what Scripture he studied that day. Fred says:

> Praying has now become an indescribable blessing, never the "chore" that it sometimes was in the past. I cannot write fast enough to keep up with my thoughts, so there is never a lag. No longer am I sending up ten-cent prayers and expecting million-dollar answers! No longer does my mind wander, as it formerly did, when I am praying. No longer do I "doze off" as has happened before, especially in the early morning.
>
> Instead of praying to God, I have found that I am often having communion with God. God has spoken to me clearly during these prayer times. . . . The writing of my prayers has also greatly deepened my love for the Lord, the sense of adoration I have for Him, my desire to praise Him at all times. Surely it has greatly strengthened my faith.

Are you challenged by Fred's words? Intrigued by the possibility of having such a vital prayer life? Then why not try it? Writing out your prayers may become a real blessing instead of a chore, and it may strengthen your faith just as it has strengthened Fred's.

Looking to God Each Day

When the children of Israel were in the wilderness, they looked to God each day for food. Likewise, we are to look to Him each day for spiritual nourishment as well as practical guidance. When we stand by our God and spend time alone with Him daily, we also find ourselves in a position to be richly blessed by Him. He wants us, His children, to look to Him daily and to walk through each day aware of His presence. A regular time of devotional reading, Bible study, and prayer is essential if we want to know God's transforming work in our lives.

As H. Norman Wright points out, a regular quiet time also helps us live according to God's will, not our own:

Create in me a pure heart, O God, and renew a steadfast spirit within me.

—Psalm 51:10

> The key to realizing the Holy Spirit's control is our will. If we are determined to do things our own way, we will continually struggle with God. We have a choice. We can live under the tyranny of our own thoughts, feelings, choices, and behaviors, or we can live under the control of the Holy Spirit. Think about it. Your choice will change your life.[7]

And, let me add that your choice to live under the control of the Holy Spirit could change your marriage! After all, it is God's Spirit which grants you the "love, joy, peace, patience, kindness, goodness, faithfulness, gentleness, self-control" that will enable you to stand by your man (Galatians 5:22-23).

Then you will call upon me
and come and pray to me,
and I will listen to you.
You will seek me and find me
when you seek me with all your
heart. I will be found by you,
declares the Lord.

—JEREMIAH 29:12–14 NIV

Prayer Requests

Date	Request	Scripture	Update/ Answer	Date
1/1	Evelyn's mother's surgery	James 5:14	Successful	1/4
1/3	The Fields' baby	Heb. 4:16	Okay	1/24
1/22	Grandma's hospital stay		Out of hospital	1/29
1/23	Pastor Foor		Better	2/5
2/3	Bevan's fever	Col. 4:2	Gone	2/6
2/20	Phil Jackson's surgery		Still some pain—keep praying	3/1

~ Sermon Notes ~

Date: *May 4* Speaker: *Pastor Don Foor*

Title: *Choose For Yourself*

Text: *Joshua 24*

Farewell address II—

A review of Israel's history

The pronoun "I" (God) is mentioned

17x's

Contrast between Israel & our growth

A. History vs. 4-5

B. Birth of a Nation vs. 6-7

C. Growth & Adolescence vs. 8-10

D. Mature Manhood vs. 11-12

E. Obedience vs. 13

F. Call for a decision vs. 14-15

(We all serve someone)

G. Response of the people vs. 16-18

H. Warning by Joshua vs. 19-24

I. Joshua makes a covenant with the people vs. 25-28

J. Joshua dies vs. 29

What is my decision?

Talents? Faith? Time?

Notes

Subject: ____________________

4

WALKING YOUR TALK

How blessed is the man who has made the LORD his trust, and has not turned to the proud, nor to those who lapse into falsehood.

—PSALM 40:4

You've probably never heard of Nicolai Pestretsov, but after you read about him, you might never forget him.

Nicolai was 36 years old, a sergeant major in the Russian army stationed in Angola. His wife had traveled the long distance from home to visit her husband when, on an August day, South African military units entered the country in quest of black nationalist guerrillas taking sanctuary there. When the South Africans encountered the Russian soldiers, four people were killed and the rest of the Russians fled—except for Sergeant Major Pestretsov.

The South African troops captured Pestretsov, and a military communique explained the situation: "Sgt. Major Nicolai Pestretsov refused to leave the body of his slain wife, who was killed in the assault on the village. He went to the body of his wife and would not leave it, although she was dead."[8]

What a picture of commitment—and what a series of questions it raises. Robert Fulghum, the teller of the story, asks these questions:

> Why didn't he run and save his own hide? What made him go back? Is it possible that he loved her? Is it possible that he wanted to hold her in his arms one last time? Is it possible that he needed to cry and grieve? Is it possible that he felt the stupidity of war? Is it possible that he felt the injustice of fate? Is it possible that he thought of children, born or unborn? Is it possible that he didn't care what became of him now? Is it possible? We don't know. Or at least we don't know for certain. But we can guess. His actions answer.[9]

What do your actions say about your commitment to your husband? What do your attitudes and words reveal about your commitment to him? Standing by the commitment you made to your spouse on your wedding day—the commitment you made before God and many witnesses—is key to a successful marriage.

Commitment to God—and to Your Spouse

Picture again Sergeant Major Pestretsov kneeling by the side of his wife's lifeless body. That level of commitment—not wanting to leave the woman to whom he'd pledged his life even when his very life was at stake—is a powerful illustration of Paul's words to husbands in Ephesus and husbands today: "Love your wives, just as Christ also loved the church and gave Himself up for her" (Ephesians 5:25). We who are married are to be as committed to our spouse as Christ is committed to the church He died for. In fact, as Christians, our marriages are to be a witness of Christ's love and grace to a watching world. Clearly, marriage is not an institution to be entered into casually.

In light of the commitment God expects in a marriage relationship, Emilie and I take very seriously the premarital counseling we do. We never, for instance, encourage two people to get married if one is a Christian and the other is not (2 Corinthians 6:14). A marriage needs to be rooted in each partner's commitment to love and serve the Lord or else the union will be divided from the start as the two people look in different directions. Besides, only a Christian marriage will result in a Christian home, and only a Christian home can glorify God and be a witness to the world.

As a young man, I had to wrestle with God's command not to marry an unbeliever. When I met Emilie, she was an unbeliever, and I knew I could not marry her. One night, as we sat on the sofa in her family's living room, I held Emilie's face in my two hands and said as firmly and lovingly as I could, "Emilie, I love you very much, but I can't ask you to marry me!"

Looking steadily into my eyes, she said quietly, "Why not?" My answer reflected the most important decision I had ever made other than accepting Jesus Christ as my personal Savior. With all the courage I could muster, I said gently, "Because you are not a Christian!"

Emilie was shocked. She had seen me as the type of man she could love and eventually marry. In her innocence, she asked me, "How do I become a Christian?" At that moment, she began to consider whether Jesus might actually be the Messiah that her Jewish people had long awaited.

It is impossible to have the feeling of peace and serenity without being at rest with God.

—Dorothy H. Pentecost

After several months of seeking answers, she prayed one evening at her bedside, "Dear God, if You have a Son and if Your Son is Jesus our Messiah, please reveal Him to me!" Emilie expected a voice to answer her immediately, but God waited a few weeks to reveal Himself to her. Then, one Sunday morning,

Emilie responded to my pastor's challenge to accept Jesus Christ as her personal Savior, and that evening she was baptized.

As I look back over our 42 years of married life, I know without any doubt that if I had married a nonbeliever, my life would have been very different. Being obedient to God resulted in being blessed by a rich and wonderful marriage rooted in His love and dedicated to Him. Furthermore, vowing before God to love Emilie through the good times and the bad reinforced my commitment to her when the times were indeed bad. Had my vows been to Emilie alone, they might have been easier to walk away from, but God's witness and the foundation He gives to Christian couples enables them to stand together no matter what comes their way.

The Words of Commitment

Perhaps your story is not that of a happy, solid marriage or of complete obedience to God's Word. Instead, you may feel very much like quitting, whether you're married to a believer or a nonbeliever. Whatever the situation, let me remind you of the vows you made before God on the day you were married, and I'll do so by means of my own experience.

When Emilie and I were married, she was 17 years old and I was 22. She was beginning her senior year in high school, and I was starting my first year of teaching. Because Emilie's family was Jewish and would not attend a Christian wedding in our church, we planned a very modest ceremony at the home of a family friend.

As we prepared for our wedding, Emilie and I were very much aware that the heart of the ceremony was to be the covenant we would enter into. We would be pledging to love one another even in our most unlovely and unlovable moments. We would be promising to stand with one another no matter what came our way on life's path.

Now it's one thing to whisper such a pledge in private, but this pledge to each other—this sacred vow—was to be made in the presence of family and friends. Before I took that important step, I wrestled with very typical questions: "Is this the right choice? Will this marriage last? Will I be able to earn enough money to support a family? Am I really ready to give up being single? Emilie is so young—are we ready to be married?" Afterward, Emilie and I both felt reassured in our decision to marry because we had received a voluntary and unconditional public commitment from one another. The wedding vows were a very special way of saying to each other, "I love you!"

I remember that ceremony as if it had happened yesterday. Pastor Robert Hubbard had us repeat the following vows:

> In the name of God, I, Bob, take you, Emilie, to be my wife; to have and to hold from this day forward; for better, for worse; for richer, for poorer; in sickness and in health; to love, honor, and cherish, until we are parted by death. This is my solemn vow.
>
> In the name of God, I, Emilie, take you, Bob, to be my husband; to have and to hold from this day forward; for better, for worse; for richer, for poorer; in sickness and in health; to love, honor, obey, and cherish, until we are parted by death. This is my solemn vow.

Again, those vows were made publicly and solemnly. More importantly, those vows were made "in the name of God." And those vows have affirmed and strengthened our love for one another for 42 years.

Couples who elope or marry in secret miss out on the dimension of community witness and celebration that can so encourage and support two newlyweds. The public pronouncement of the wedding vows before family and friends helps to remind a couple that their marriage involves something more than just two people who love each other. Emilie and I also knew that our wedding had a sacred and eternal significance. When we made our vows before God, we were saying to each other and to all the witnesses that God is the source of our love and that the purpose of our life together is to do His will and serve Him.

After Emilie and I stated our vows to each other, the pastor made this pronouncement: "Those whom God has joined together, let no man put asunder. For as much as you, Bob and Emilie, have consented together in this sacred covenant and have declared the same before God and this company of friends, I pronounce you husband and wife. In the name of the Father and of the Son and of the Holy Spirit. Amen."

Learn to commit your soul and the building of it to One who can keep it and build it as you never can.

—P.T. FORSYTH

I had vowed before God, before Emilie, and before many witnesses to love and cherish my new wife. Through the years, I have come back again and again to those words of commitment that I spoke at 6:45 P.M. on Friday, September 30, 1955. They have served as a powerful reminder of our commitment before God, which is the foundation of our marriage.

In the years since that day, I have been very glad that God blessed our lives with those vows. They have been a signpost of the significance of marriage before God and kept us together when feelings of love momentarily waned and the challenges of life seemed as if they would overwhelm us.

I share at length my own experience in hopes of encouraging you to reflect on your vows and to stand by that commitment you made to your husband. May God graciously remind you of the solemn pledge you made on your wedding day and of the fact that you made that vow not only to your husband, but also to God.

MARRIAGE VOWS FOR TODAY

Now imagine for a moment that your wedding is taking place today. If you were to rewrite the vows you spoke however many years ago, what would you promise to do? What commitments would you make? Thinking through your commitment to your husband in a fresh, new way can do much to revitalize your commitment to him. Consider the following statements other couples have written:

- "My commitment to you is to listen to your concerns each day for the purpose of having the kind of marriage we both want."
- "I realize that our love will change. I will work to maintain a high level of romance, courtship, and love in our relationship."
- "I pledge myself to confront problems when they arise and not retreat like a turtle hiding in its shell."
- "I commit myself to you in times of joy and in times of problems. We will tackle and share our problems together."
- "I promise that I will never be too busy to look at the flowers with you."
- "I will respect any beliefs and capabilities that are different from mine and will not attempt to make you into a copy of me."
- "I will be open and honest with no secrets, and I desire you to be the same with me."
- "I will reflect the Word of God in my relationship with you."[10]

Now take a few minutes to write out some vows for your marriage. You'll find this a wonderful exercise for your husband to do, too. When the time is right—perhaps on your wedding anniversary or during a quiet weekend alone—share your rewritten and updated vows with one another. Discuss them and recommit your marriage to God. You'll find that these vows—written by two people who now have a real-life understanding of marriage—can give renewed meaning and purpose to your marriage.

After the Wedding

Several years ago, our friends Fred and Florence Littauer wrote the bestselling book *After Every Wedding Comes a Marriage*, and that title reflects a truth that engaged couples can't fully appreciate. There's a difference between being a bride or groom in a wedding and being a husband or wife in a marriage. That truth was in our minds as Emilie and I watched our two children make plans for their large church weddings. The wedding ceremony is only the beginning; it's afterward that the couple faces the real challenges. We knew all too well that a beautiful wedding is no indication that the marriage that follows will be beautiful.

> *A happy marriage is the union of two good forgivers.*
>
> —Robert Quillen

Perhaps you were caught by surprise when you first began to realize how difficult marriage can be. After all, none of us can ever really know what it means to be married until we are married. Consequently, we can find that return from the honeymoon a rather rude awakening to the very real challenges of two people becoming one and learning to live together. Those day-to-day challenges can indeed test the words of commitment we spoke to each other on that special day of music and lace and love.

Tragically, we live in an age when commitment doesn't mean what it did a few decades ago. All around us and in a variety of contexts—sports, business, politics, and even the family—we see people break their promises and walk away from their commitments. A person's word is no longer binding the way it once was.

It's also possible for our commitments to be weakened by the world's message that we can "have it all." This lie from Satan encourages people to look for something better rather than be content or try to improve what they already have. Broken marriages, families, and people result when we walk away from the vows we made to one another and before God.

This lie, with its implication that we can and should be happy, also sows seeds of dissatisfaction with life. As I look around today, I see individuals and couples who are not content with their lives. The apostle Paul, however, learned to be content no matter what his circumstances—and his circumstances were sometimes very difficult (Philippians 4:11). Paul knew beatings, stonings, imprisonment, shipwreck, hunger, sleeplessness, cold, and danger from rivers, robbers, and false brethren (2 Corinthians 11:23-27). Paul's commitment to the Lord kept him strong despite the hardships, and your commitment to the Lord—spoken in your wedding vows—can keep you strong in your marriage.

Paul knew God to be the source of real staying power and true contentment, and we must turn to God, too, as we face the unfairness, evil, and hardship of the world. We can be content in Christ despite the hunger, wars, killings, disease, earthquakes, tornadoes, hurricanes, floods, fires, robberies, and social and civil injustices of our fallen world. Closer to home, we can be content in Christ despite the challenges, demands, and even empty times of marriage. Paul proclaimed, "I can do all things through Him who strengthens me" (Philippians 4:13), and you can claim that promise from God for yourself in your marriage. The God before whom you vowed to love your husband will enable you to stand by him.

Your Marriage and the Gospel

Susannah Wesley, the mother of the eighteenth-century evangelist John Wesley, once observed, "There are two things to do about the gospel—believe it and behave it." The easier part is to believe it; the harder part is to behave it. And that may be true of your wedding

Expressions of Love

- Pack a bag of his favorite cookies and put it in his suitcase before he leaves on a trip. Insert a little note expressing how much you miss him.
- Go out for dessert together.
- Give him a coupon he can redeem for a leg rub.
- Give him coffee, tea, or hot chocolate in an insulated car mug for his drive to work.
- Let him choose the thermostat setting tonight.

vows: The easier part is to believe the promises you made; the harder part is to act on those promises. When we do act on those promises, however, we show the world how much we believe the gospel and our marriage vows. Marriage—with its stresses, trials, and inescapable closeness to another person—is certainly a test to see how we live out the gospel. In marriage, for instance, we have every opportunity to share the fruit of the Spirit with our spouse (Galatians 5:22,23). All that God asks us to do and be as His son or daughter can be—and should be—worked out within a marriage relationship. Christian stewardship is also an issue in the arena of marriage: God will ask whether Emilie is a better Christian for having been married to me.

It's easy to love when you are loved, and give when you receive . . . but the truest love springs in response to those who are in need.

—FRANK CARPENTER

When we honor our vows, marriage can indeed be a wonderful blessing. Consider George Eliot's perspective on the marriage union:

> What greater thing is there for two human souls than to feel that they are joined for life—to strengthen each other in all labor, to rest in each other in all sorrow, to minister to each other in all pain, to be one with each other in silent unspeakable memories at the moment of the last parting."[11]

May God help you believe these words anew, and may He richly bless you as you live them out.

5

A Gentle, Quiet Spirit

"For I know the plans I have for you," declares the LORD*, "plans to prosper you and not to harm you, plans to give you hope and a future.*

—JEREMIAH 29:11 NIV

Let me assure you that men love to be in the presence of a real lady. Such a woman makes men feel more masculine, more self-confident, and more relaxed. A real lady affects us not just because of how she looks or dresses, but also because of who she is.

What do I mean by a "real lady"? A woman who worked in our local bank for years comes to mind. As she dealt with her customers, she radiated peace. She always offered tranquillity, warmth, friendliness, courtesy, and a welcoming spirit. In a woman, these traits can be very feminine, and men respond favorably. The apostle Peter offered this perspective on femininity: "Let not your adornment be merely external . . . but let it be the hidden person of the heart, with the imperishable quality of a gentle and quiet spirit, which is precious in the sight of God" (1 Peter 3:3,4).

What is *feminine*? It's not a particular style, form, dress, or interior decorating. *Feminine* encompasses an infinite variety of physical appearances. It is a softness, gentleness, and graciousness that men don't have. A woman can be the president of a corporation or be a tough and aggressive participant in the business world and still be feminine. To me, feminine also means that a woman has a sense of who she is apart from what she does. She nurtures a strong spirituality, and manifests the fruit of the Spirit in every aspect of her life (see Galatians 5:22,23). Femininity also brings to my mind a deep concern for her husband and children, the ability to submit to her husband when appropriate (Ephesians 5:22), and the maternal awareness that she is raising not only her children but generations to come. A truly feminine woman understands the mystique of being a godly wife and mother.

A gentle and quiet spirit, tranquillity, being at peace, sharing the fruit of the Spirit with people—these qualities are a direct result of a woman's relationship with God.[12] When a woman is right with God, she doesn't feel any need to prove herself. Confident in herself and aware of her God-given strengths, she doesn't feel compelled to use those strengths to control other people. She enjoys an inner contentment that isn't based on accomplishments, status, authority, power, or other people's opinions.

A woman who walks closely with God is free from aggressiveness and the need to prove her worth. Although, she may be competitive and very energetic by temperament, she is affirmed not by other people but by her God. Such a woman "opens her mouth in wisdom, and the teaching of kindness is on her tongue" (Proverbs 31:26), and her family is

---

Apples of Gold

A fitly spoken word
Will turn much wrath away;
It can be said and heard,
Without a great display.
And every spoken word
Can gladden and portray
A feeling that will gird
For living by the day.

—Clyde S. Creel

---

blessed. "The heart of her husband trusts in her, and he will have no lack of gain. She does him good and not evil all the days of her life. . . . Her children rise up and bless her" (Proverbs 31:11,12,28). A gracious, feminine woman doesn't try to attain greatness for herself, but, instead, she is an inspiration to her husband and helps him rise to his own greatness. She supports him unconditionally in his search for fulfillment and achievement. And such a woman—one closely in tune with God—is indeed worthy of praise as she models godly values and high moral standards and truly reflects the feminine virtues of patience, silence, and faith. A woman's gentle and quiet spirit makes her a blessing to the people around her.

Gentleness, patience, and devotion to God—the components of godly femininity—are qualities that hold society together and provide hope for the future. History shows that as the woman goes, so goes the family. You give meaning and purpose to a home. You are the heartbeat, pumping vital blood into the family system by setting the spirit and tone of the home. Your softer, more feminine qualities help set the atmosphere of the home. You help your husband and children establish and live by moral standards.

The femininity I have described teaches, inspires, and civilizes. It brings glory to God and hope to His world. And, on a less tangible or practical level, such femininity also has a real mystique about it—but many women don't capitalize on this. Their grandmothers—who were students of men and knew what made men tick and what made them ticked!—knew how their feminity affected men.

Pastor John was a minister and an avid reader who spent large amounts of time in the library studying and preparing for the next Sunday's sermon. One mother wise about the practical aspects of a gracious wife offered this advice to her future daughter-in-law: "John loves to study and often works late into the night at the library. Don't try to change him, but always have his dinner in a warm oven and keep a pot of coffee on the stove." The young lady listened to her future mother-in-law and, at last account, she had been married to Pastor John for over 40 years.

Pastor John's wife truly understood the magic of being a woman. As the Living Bible puts it, she was an example of "that kind of deep beauty . . . seen in the saintly women of old who trusted God and fitted in with their husbands' plans" (1 Peter 3:5 TLB). This type of woman can be irresistible to men. Even twentieth-century women acknowledge the mystique of womanhood. Consider what Dr. Toni Grant wrote in *Being a Woman*: "It is women to whom men look to bring out their gentler natures and their highest ideals, inflame their passions, and motivate them to achievement. This feminine woman is a rarity in today's culture, and the traditional male still seeks valiantly for her inspiration."[13] Even today, the mystique can work. Are you letting it work for you to enrich your marriage?

The Call to Submission

Perhaps the idea of using the magic of being feminine sounds quite old-fashioned. To introduce yet another "old-fashioned" idea, let me ask you a few questions about your family role. Are you tired of being a leader? Do you often find yourself forcing your ideas onto others, being overly assertive, always choosing how to discipline the children, or deciding where to go on vacation? Are you wanting to become more feminine—to nurture a gentle and quiet spirit and a deeper devotion to the Lord? Are you wondering how to gain or regain that feminine mystique that can enrich your marriage? I think the best way for a woman to become more feminine is to become less masculine. This might seem out of step with the times, but it is based on guidelines given by our wise and loving God.

I suggest that you consider the truth of the old adage, "Opposites attract." In the light of this age-old wisdom, I propose that one way you can help your husband stand strong in his masculinity is to be firm in your femininity.

Women can use their femininity to magnetize and encourage their man. They don't—as many women today do—play the traditional male game of "The Quest." They don't run after a man, manipulate the situation, capture him, and then leave when they find themselves no longer interested in him. Instead, a woman who is comfortable being feminine, will draw a man to her like a magnet attracts iron filings. In marriage, too, your femininity can draw your husband to you. Your confidence, your security in who you are as a woman and a child of God, and your feminine mystique will serve as a magnet. So develop that mystery, don't be predictable, and allow your husband to pursue you. If you keep your husband guessing, he'll find himself thinking about you, missing you, and wanting to be with you. Also, keep learning more about how to use your feminine ways to engage and excite your husband. Change your hair, try a new perfume, or kidnap him for a special romantic weekend. You'll enrich your husband's life and free him to be more masculine.

God created men and women in His image. One is not superior to the other; they are equal and complementary. Our different functions within marriage have nothing to do with superiority or inferiority. Instead, equality in our Creator God's eyes calls both husbands and wives to mutual respect and affirmation based on the awareness that we are created in God's image and, as fellow believers, are called to "be subject to one another in the fear of Christ" (Ephesians 5:21). This passage is one of Emilie's and my favorite marriage verses. Each day as we wake we ask ourselves, "How can I be submissive to my mate today? Can I run an errand, go to the hardware store, the cleaners, the grocery store? Can I babysit the children?" Many such ways express true love to a husband or wife.

In Ephesians 5:22-23, a well-known but often misunderstood passage on marriage, we find God's instructions on leadership in the home. The passage reads: "You wives must submit to your husbands' leadership in the same way you submit to the Lord" (TLB). Remember, this is not a plan developed by a human being—it was given to us by God. Why? Because it really works! When wives submit to their husbands in the same way they submit to the Lord, a marriage can be spared power plays, conflicts, and indecision.

Many women today have a difficult time with the word submission. I define submission simply as "arranging oneself under the authority of another." If your husband asks you to do something contrary to a moral or biblical principle, I don't believe you must submit to his leadership. But I do believe that biblical submission calls for a wife to trust, respect, and honor her husband. When women harbor resentment, resistance, or rebellion, love can't grow. Furthermore, as Toni Grant asserts, "women are best able to live out their feminine aspects when they give over some of their male dominance to the opposite sex freely and unconditionally. When a woman is willing to do this, she inspires enormous confidence in her man and enhances not only his masculinity, but her own femininity as well."[14]

Becoming More Feminine

Femininity doesn't mean all women are to act the same. The specific expressions of femininity vary greatly. When Emilie thinks "feminine," she usually thinks of soft colors, lace, and flowers. She loves ruffled curtains and flower-sprigged wallpaper, delicate bone china, and old-fashioned garden prints. She feels especially beautiful when she's dressed in soft and colorful fabrics.

In recent years we have been obsessed with figuring out what a woman should be allowed to do. God says in his Word a woman can do anything; the point is not what she does but what she is.

— Anne Ortlund

But there are women with vastly different styles who still exude that special quality of femininity—women who wear their tailored tweeds or their casual cottons (or their gardening "grubbies") with an air of gentleness and sensitivity. Women who fill their sleek modern kitchens or their utilitarian offices with that unmistakable sense of warmth, caring, and responsiveness. Women who combine self-confidence and an indomitable spirit with a gracious humility and a tender teachability.

The spirit of femininity is so many things. It includes choosing objects for their beauty as well as their usefulness . . . and lovingly caring for them. It is people accepted and nurtured, loveliness embraced and shared. More important, the spirit of femininity is the spirit of care and compassion. The most feminine woman is one with an eye and ear for others and a heart for God.

What activities help you feel more feminine?

A Feminine Serenity

The dictionary defines *serene* as "calm, clear, unruffled, peaceful, placid, tranquil, [and] unperturbed." Do those words describe anyplace or anyone you know? Maybe the Grand Canyon? And maybe a wise woman who has discovered the peace of our Lord and learned how to rest in Him? That dictionary definition of *serene* describes so few places and people in today's world. We have fast-food restaurants, drive-through lines, car phones, second-day mail, next-day mail, and facsimile machines—at home and even in the car!

Order and the beauty of peace go together. The fair flower of peace does not grow among the weeds of an ill-regulated life. The radiance of a deep inner serenity is the product of disciplining both in the heart and in outward affairs.

—G.H. Morling

We yearn for peace and quiet, but where do we turn? We must turn to God. We have to become quiet inside. Chuck Swindoll comments about the quietness we need today:

> You know something? That still, small voice will never shout. God's methods don't change because we are so noisy and busy. He is longing for your attention, your

> undivided and full attention. He wants to talk with you in times of quietness (with the TV off) about your need for understanding, love, compassion, patience, self-control, a calm spirit, genuine humility . . . and wisdom. But He won't run to catch up. He will wait and wait until you finally sit in silence and listen.[15]

We need to be quiet before the Lord, to experience His peace and His restoring touch. We need to listen to what He would teach us and hear where He would have us go. We will benefit greatly from such times with our heavenly Father. Your peaceful calm will be restored.

A man responds well to a woman who is serene. She settles the environment just by her presence; she is at peace with those around her. A serene woman is sensitive to nature, aware of all aspects of her womanhood, and willing to help make the world better. Furthermore, she is not so rushed that she can't give her husband and family her time. Her home will reflect this serenity, encouraging people to relax. Guests will ask, "How do you ever leave this home? It's so comfortable! I feel such tranquillity when I'm with you, and it's so good to relax." Has anyone told you this lately?

"A woman without serenity seems hardly a woman at all; she is nervous, high-strung, all 'bent out of shape' and utterly impatient,"[16] believes Toni Grant.

Expressions of Love

- Buy some new lingerie for tonight—or that weekend getaway!
- Bake a batch of chocolate chip cookies for your family.
- Greet your husband at the door with a kiss.
- Make your home a special place to be: buy fresh or silk flowers; use soft, gentle-smelling potpourri, and so on.
- Create a pleasing, romantic aroma for your mate by lingering in a bathtub spiced with fragrant oils.

One key to finding serenity is learning to let life happen around you. You don't have to be involved in everything. Sometimes it is very right to say no. Let go of those things you can't control. Serenity and tranquillity are gifts from God. They come when we trust Him as our Lord, Shepherd, Guide, and Protector.

Becoming Serene

Despite how different our world is from early America, a wife and mother *can* make her home a place of serenity. It starts when she discovers and nurtures the serenity that God alone gives. Here are some ways to develop a serenity that will weather the demands of being a wife and mother.

- Sit in a quiet room for 5, 10, or 15 minutes, and reflect on what God is doing in your life. Wait upon the Lord. Listen for Him to direct, encourage, guide, and teach you.
- Hold hands with your husband and think about God's love, power, and peace. Tell your husband that you love him.
- Turn on some peaceful music.
- Take a walk at the beach, on a mountain trail, or in a snowy meadow. Ski down a hill or watch the leaves fall off the trees.
- Take a warm bubble bath.
- Say no to someone who wants you to do something that would keep you away from your family.
- Don't volunteer for anything new for two weeks.
- Speak quietly and smile when you talk.
- Keep a journal of your daily events and feelings.

I challenge and encourage you to try some of these activities. See if you don't discover a new sense of serenity. Then observe how serenity affects your husband, your children, and your home.

Being a woman is such a privilege. Your femininity is a gift you can give to your husband, your children, and the other people around you. Your gentle touch can warm up a cold, no-nonsense atmosphere with an aura of "I care." Women have the ability to transform an environment—to make it comfortable and inviting. If you rejoice in that ability and make the most of it, your husband will certainly be attracted to the fragrance of your life.

The Walls of Home

The walls of home, like galleries,
hold pictures rich and rare;
All framed in golden memories,
and kept with loving care.
Some tableaux echo childish glee,
and others are serene;
While love, and faith, and loyalty
illumine every scene.
Tho' years may alter museum halls,
and banish transient arts,
The timeless joys within home's
walls are etched on human
hearts.

—Ann Brannon,
Home Life, May 1956

What Makes a Man Feel Loved

6

Becoming a Suitable Helpmate

Then the Lord God said, "It is not good for the man to be alone; I will make him a helper suitable for him."

—Genesis 2:18

"Bob, would you mind helping me move this table? I'm not strong enough!" I love to hear Emilie say that she needs me. Her need allows me to be what God created me to be: the stronger partner, the protector, the provider. If I'm not allowed to help my wife, one of my purposes as a husband and a man is taken away from me.

Men love to help—especially in emergency situations. A few years ago Southern California had seven days of torrential rain—at one point receiving six inches in a six-hour period. Rushing waters washed over cars, and 40 people had to be helicoptered to safety. Teenagers were swept away when normally dry riverbeds became swollen and powerful rivers. Mud slides destroyed homes and lives. And in all these situations men risked their lives trying to help people in need. The media reported numerous tales of how men offered their assistance despite the danger. When there is a need, men respond! Just like a truck driver who stops alongside the freeway to assist a stranded motorist, a man who recognizes a need or hears it expressed will respond. We simply have to know we're needed.

But Who Needs Help?

In our Western culture, however, we consider ourselves very capable. We pride ourselves on our self-sufficiency and ability to get things done. We don't need help from anyone! And that is as true for women as it is for men.

Many women today are hard-charging, assertive, and very competent. The wise woman of the 90s, however, is beginning to slow down. She has realized that enough's enough, and she is giving up her attempt to be superwoman and/or supermom. She has realized that the elusive goal of doing and being all things isn't worth what it's costing her to try to reach it. Such a woman, free of society's unrealistic expectations and its call to be independent, can say "Honey, I need you. Would you please help me?"

Show Him You Need Him

One way to melt a man's heart is to show him that you truly need him. The simple, direct statement, "I need your help" reinforces your husband's masculinity. Most husbands won't refuse a wife's straightforward expression of a need:

- "Will you please help me with this lamp?"
- "Would you hold me while I cry? It's so hard to see my mother suffering. . . ."
- "Please help me figure out what the instructor wants here."
- "Could we go to the beach this weekend—just the two of us? I need some time with you."

Whether your request is large or small, ask your husband for help. The way life goes, you won't have to make up opportunities for him to help you. We all have plenty of very real needs that can be expressed.

In her book *Being a Woman*, clinical psychologist Toni Grant offers wives this advice:

> It is important that a man feels that he fulfills a purpose in your life, that he somehow makes the woman feel better, safer, and more beautiful than she was before. He needs to know that his masculine presence makes a difference to her feminine well being; otherwise two people may have met person to person, but not man to woman.[17]

Scripture also teaches the importance of having someone there to help us when we are in need. The writer of Ecclesiastes notes that "two are better than one because they have a good return for their labor. For if either of them falls, the one will lift up his companion. But woe to the one who falls when there is not another to lift him up" (4:9,10). In Galatians 6:2, Paul calls believers to "bear one another's burdens, and thus fulfill the law of Christ." Again and again, Scripture reminds us of the importance of having someone come alongside to help when times are difficult. Reaching out helps our needs to be met and also creates a special bond with the person we let come near.

I encourage you to let your husband come near, whether your need is large or small, emotional, physical, spiritual, intellectual, or material. One of his key roles is to provide for and protect his family. When you allow your husband to do this you bring out his masculine side. You'll probably also find yourself feeling closer to him because he has just taken care of you in some way.

Knowing and Meeting Your Mate's Needs

Women and men are often unaware of what their partners need. Why are we so blind? Perhaps because some of us are looking for what we can get, rather than what we can give in our marriage. Most of us are more than willing and ready to give—but we don't know what to give or how we can best meet our mate's needs. In fact, after 42 years of marriage, Emilie and I are still trying to figure this one out!

In *His Needs, Her Needs*, author Willard F. Harley, Jr., lists five basic needs husbands and wives bring to a marriage:

Men's Needs	**Women's Needs**
1. Sexual fulfillment	1. Affection
2. Recreational companionship	2. Conversation
3. An attractive spouse	3. Honesty and openness
4. Domestic support	4. Financial support
5. Admiration	5. Family commitment[18]

Recognizing and meeting these needs for one another will mean a stronger marriage and the ability to get through the rocky times that come. A wife benefits greatly when her husband recognizes her needs and does his best to meet them—without always having to be asked! In keeping with the purpose of this book, though, I will focus on a husband's needs and how you can meet them.

Sexual Fulfillment

Our society is bombarded with it from the cereal boxes we see in the morning to the moisturizing lotions we use at night. We see it everywhere we look—from magazines to newspapers, from radio to television, from the advertising on gigantic billboards to the advertising posted on the sides of city buses. Billions of dollars each year are spent by manufacturers using it to persuade you and me to purchase their products. The "it," of course, is sex. Everywhere we turn we are confronted with sexy women and lusty men who are trying to influence us by promising that a certain brand of car, underwear, toothpaste, or soft drink will fulfill our needs for love, sex, and intimacy.

In Emilie's background, sexual intimacy was synonymous with a dull, dirty duty. Her home, dominated by a violent alcoholic father, was anything but a model of romantic love, fulfilling sex, or warm intimacy between a husband and wife. According to Emilie's early view, sex was something a couple did to have children. It was not something which was pleasurable or enjoyable. When her father died, Emilie was left without a father figure for the important teenage years of her life. So she came to our marriage without a healthy understanding of the role of love, sex, and intimacy between a husband and wife. She was first attracted to me by the gentleness and warmth which she had missed in her home, but she didn't have a positive model from home as a point of reference for developing intimacy in our relationship.

Contrary to Emilie's experience, I was brought up by very gentle, loving parents. There were always positive expressions of love around. Sex was much more to our parents than just creating children. It was a topic that was discussed with great respect. My parents were very open with their hugs, kisses, compliments, and physical "love" pinches. They started their romancing early in the day and were ready to show the world how much they loved each other.

So on the topic of love, sex, and intimacy, Emilie and I were examples of the axiom that opposites attract. We entered our marriage relationship from two opposite poles, as different as hot and cold. And yet here we are, well into our fourth decade together as husband and wife, and more in love now than when we started. I could have "rushed and crushed"

How do I love thee?
Let me count the ways.
I love thee to the depth
and breadth and height
My soul can reach, when
feeling out of sight
For the ends of Being
and ideal Grace.
I love thee to the level of
everyday's
Most quiet need, by sun
and candlelight.
I love thee freely, as men
strive for Right:
I love thee purely, as
they turn from Praise.
I love thee with the passion put to use
In my old griefs, and
with my childhood's faith.
I love thee with a love I
seemed to lose
With my lost saints—I
love thee with the breath,
Smiles, tears, of all my
life—and, if God choose,
I shall but love thee
better after death.

—ELIZABETH BARRETT BROWNING

Emilie with my sexuality and openness; and she could have iced our relationship from her background that lacked intimacy. But with love, trust, and patience on both our parts, our relationship has grown into the loving, intimate partnership we enjoy today.

In order to promote an atmosphere of love and mutual fulfillment, we need to foster romance in our marriages. Are you a romantic wife? If not, start making phone calls to say, "I love you." Leave sexy notes for him and send thoughtful cards expressing your love in tender words. Give your mate physical attention: Hold hands, touch tenderly, hug and kiss often. If your mate comes from a home that was less affectionate than yours, patiently grow together as physically romantic partners by lovingly teaching each other the magic of touch.

And women, it's okay for you to initiate sexual intimacy. God gave women as well as men the desire for sex, so it makes sense that at times you will initiate the intimacy. In fact, Emilie has planned some of our most exciting and romantic evenings. Sometimes, for instance, she prepares a "love basket." She takes a large basket lined with a lacy tablecloth and fills it with our favorite foods, sparkling cider, a candle, and even a bunch of fresh flowers. The setting for the meal can be in the park, at the beach, at an outdoor concert, or in the bedroom with candlelight and soft music. (There is a complete chapter on the "love basket" in Emilie's book *More Hours in My Day*.) Romance like this promotes an atmosphere of love and leads to mutual fulfillment, sexual and otherwise.

> *We pray that the young men and women of today and tomorrow will grow up with the realization that sex is a beautiful flame they carry in the lantern of their bodies.*
>
> —Demetrius Monousos

There are many ways you can add romance to your marriage. Send flowers or make a phone call to say, "I love you." Leave a sexy note for your mate or send a card that expresses your love. Give your mate physical attention. (Be patient if your mate comes from a home that wasn't as openly affectionate as yours.) Romance leads to emotional intimacy, a key contributor to sexual intimacy.

Another key to sexual fulfillment has to do with the sexual act itself. Having achieved emotional intimacy, many Christian couples wonder what kind of sexual intimacy is appropriate for believers. Again and again Emilie and I are asked, "Is it okay for Christian couples to . . . ?" In response, we usually refer to Hebrews 13:4: "Let marriage be held in honor among all, and let the marriage bed be undefiled," as the guideline to determine what kind of lovemaking is appropriate. Emilie and I talk to each other to see if the activity in question would enrich our intimacy. If we both feel that the activity would bring us closer together, and if both of us would enjoy it, we go ahead.

Sometimes a couple puts a certain lovemaking technique on hold because one partner is uncomfortable with the idea, and that is as it should be. We must be very sensitive to our partner's desires and not pressure him or her into doing something uncomfortable. After all, our sexuality is a gift given to promote intimacy! If you aren't sure about certain practices, apply the principle of Proverbs 3:6: "In all thy ways acknowledge him, and he shall direct thy paths" (KJV). Talk to the Lord about the proposed activity. It's amazing how God will reveal the proper answer for both of you.

Husbands and wives experience sexual fulfillment when emotional intimacy has already been achieved, when we agree on appropriate activities, and—the third key—when we are students of our mates and therefore able to meet their needs. What better way to learn what our mate needs and enjoys than to ask questions and discuss feelings, needs, and expectations? Emilie doesn't hesitate to ask me if there is anything I would like her to do for me sexually that we aren't doing or if there is anything that I don't want her to do—and I freely ask her the same questions. Such frank discussions can eliminate assumptions and pave the way for deeper intimacy and greater sexual fulfillment. When Emilie tells me where she likes to be touched and stroked, I can more completely meet her needs and enrich our lovemaking.

Let me add a few more thoughts on sexual intimacy. I encourage you and your husband to alternate the roles of giver and receiver in foreplay and intercourse. Don't get into a rut. Keep some mystery in your sex life. The sex act alone—without romantic moments, open communication, and mutual contentment in the relationship—can become shallow and lonely. Express through verbal and nonverbal communication your wants and preferences and encourage your husband to do the same. Sex in a context of openness, trust, acceptance, and love is indeed rich and fulfilling for both partners.

God's Idea of Intimacy

The Bible's teaching on marriage has helped Emilie and me learn about God's master plan for husbands and wives. One of the most important passages we have discovered is 1 Corinthians 7:1-5:

> It is good for a man not to touch a woman. But because of immoralities, let each man have his own wife, and let each woman have her own husband. Let the husband fulfill his duty to his wife, and likewise also the wife to her husband. The wife does not have authority over her own body, but the husband does; and likewise also the husband does not have authority over his own body, but the wife does. Stop depriving one another, except by agreement for a time that you may devote yourselves to prayer, and come together again lest Satan tempt you because of your lack of self-control.

These verses provide four solid guidelines for couples who desire love and intimacy in their relationship.

First, be faithful to one person. Sexual immorality was rampant in the city of Corinth, the home of the church to which Paul is writing here—and our society is, sadly, quite similar to that ancient world. Christian men and women today live in a world that accepts extramarital affairs and divorce.

Places of employment and the local gym are often scenes of temptation. God's Word, however, clearly commands us to be faithful to our spouse (Exodus 20:14; Matthew 5:27-32; 19:18).

Second, be available to each other. A husband is to give of himself to fulfill his wife's needs, and a wife is to give of herself to fulfill her husband's needs. We are to freely ask for and give affection to one another. Don't be afraid to tell your mate that you are in the mood for love. Always be ready to respond when your partner is in the mood. If you are too tired to enjoy each other and meet each other's needs, you may need to eliminate other commitments and activities in order to be the kind of spouse God calls you to be.

Third, submit to each other. Closely related to being available to our partners is being willing to submit to their sexual desires and needs. Wives, if your mate wants to make love, you should not withhold yourself from him, but submit to his desires. Be open about your own desires and your energy level so you can arrive at a mutually satisfying plan for the evening. Be aware, too, that your willingness to meet your partner's sexual needs and desires—besides being an act of obedience to Scripture—may very well prevent him from falling into sin with someone who seems more ready to meet his needs than you are.

Marriage is a sacred vow or commitment that you both made before God, and it is a very serious matter to break that vow. God gave marriage to us for our happiness, and I believe with his help you can discover what it means to build your lives together on Christ's foundation.

—BILLY GRAHAM

Finally, keep on meeting your spouse's sexual needs. Paul notes that the only exception to this guideling is taking time for prayer and fasting. Other than those specified times, a husband and wife should be available to each other and always seek to meet the other's needs.

The Bible offers rich insight into the marriage relationship. Consider, for instance, that the New Testament writers liken Jesus' relationship to the church to the relationship between a husband and wife (see Ephesians 5:25). I encourage you to spend some time studying what God's Word teaches about your marriage. Knowing and following the Creator's master plan will enrich your marriage—sexually and otherwise.

Intimate Tips for Women

When Emilie talks to women about how to build intimacy in their marriages, she often directs them to the teachings of 1 Peter 3:1-6. Whether or not your husband is a believer, Emilie says, he will respond favorably if you follow these scriptural guidelines:

- Be submissive to your husband. Don't resist him or rebel against him.
- Demonstrate your Christian faith through your lifestyle. Don't preach.
- Be loyal to your husband in every way.
- Take care to remain attractive on the outside.
- Develop a quiet and gentle spirit that is inwardly attractive.
- Develop a feminine and serene style to your life.

I would add that a woman should never criticize or attack her husband. A man's outward display of strength—however irritating that display may be—is often a cover-up for feelings of insecurity. When a woman attacks her man's ego, she certainly doesn't foster the intimacy she desires in the relationship. Instead, her husband may become withdrawn and noncommunicative, angry, and resentful. He won't respond to his critical wife with sensitivity, understanding, and compassion, and he may find himself unable to perform sexually. Also, he may easily be tempted to infidelity by a woman who understands his needs and will build up rather than tear him down. So rather than attack your husband, respect him and encourage him. Your husband needs to know that he is important to you and your children. When he knows you believe in him and support him, he will be much more open and ready to be intimate with you.

Is Intimacy Possible?

Are you wondering whether real intimacy is even possible in your marriage? I assure you that it is. Genuine intimacy comes when both you and your husband are willing to submit yourselves to each other out of reverence for Christ (see Ephesians 5:21). For 42 years, such mutual submission has protected Emilie and me from Satan who would have based his attacks on a prideful unwillingness to bend, accommodate, and submit to one another.

Know, too, that intimacy doesn't just happen. It takes persistent prayer and discipline to apply God's principles that encourage intimacy to your marriage. Again, I challenge you to study God's Word on your own and with your spouse to learn what He says about love, sex, and intimacy.

I also challenge you to look at yourself as honestly as you can. What qualities would make you a better wife? Where is God calling you to welcome His transforming Spirit into your heart? Ask God to help you see where you can become more the wife He wants you to be. Then prayerfully set some goals for yourself and pursue them doggedly.

Finally, continue to love the Lord with all your heart. By actively loving God and walking closely with Him, you plug yourself into His infinite and divine love, which will feed your love for your husband and foster intimacy in your marriage. Be a doer of the Word in your marriage. Let your obedience to God's commands to serve and to love one another bring new life and new closeness to your marriage. After all, God created sex and marriage, and He desires that you find love and intimacy in His creation.

Recreational Companionship

We've spent a lot of time looking at the item that tops the list of what men need. Sexual fulfillment is indeed important, but now let's move on to the next need we men have: recreational companionship. Think back to those early courting days. Do you have memories of tennis, golf, hiking, camping, sporting events, and Laker's basketball? Now that you have been married a few years and have a child or two, have you stopped doing those things? Or maybe your husband still enjoys those activities, but you are happier reading books, listening to good music, watching a good romance movie on television, or spending an evening at the theater. Or maybe you're the athlete and your husband prefers more sedentary activities. Do you remember how you and your husband used to love doing everything together? Is that still true? Or are you wondering what went wrong along the way?

Think about those couples you know who seem to have a strong marriage. They almost certainly exhibit an ability to enjoy each other's interests. And that doesn't mean that she plays tennis only and always with him or that he won't go out on the golf course without her. It means that spouses are interested and supportive of each other's recreation.

Our son, Brad, for instance, married a woman who likes to run, swim, bicycle, exercise, and sweat just as he does. Maria participates in many of his recreational activities. In our case, however, Emilie is not very athletic, but she does encourage and support my interest in sports. Likewise, I spend time with her doing what she enjoys—going out to dinner to celebrate a special occasion, attending the theater, or reading a book together. Emilie and I work together to give each other the freedom to enjoy our personal interests *and* to enjoy what the other person likes. Such compromise and sharing of our time keeps us growing together, something that separate vacations and long-term or frequent solo outings would not allow. In fact, such separateness can be very dangerous to a marriage relationship—and separateness isn't even what we men always want.

Although the media shows the boys out fishing, drinking beer, and saying, "It doesn't get better than this!" we men do want our wives to share fun and recreational activities with us. Certainly many men's activities may be riskier, sweatier, and dirtier than women enjoy, and some women's activities may be too quiet or passive for men. Emilie's choice of a movie, for instance, reflects her preference for softness, romance, and tenderness. I don't receive the same response to an invitation to a Clint Eastwood movie that I do when I ask her to see a romance! Again, compromise is called for, as is balance, and recreational compromises might include lunch or dinner out, a picnic, a walk, shopping, and attending various cultural events.

At times, however, men need to be with men and women need to be with women. After all, we have different needs and we have different things to give to one another. I'm sure you know the satisfaction of "girl talk." No matter how good a listener your husband is, there is something qualitatively different about sharing the latest event with a special friend. She gives you something that your husband can't give and meets a need that your husband can't meet. Likewise, some of my male friends give me things that Emilie can't and, in doing so, meet some of my needs that Emilie can't meet (through no fault of her own). It's a fact of life that our mate is not going to meet all our needs. That's why same-sex friendships are so important to a healthy marriage.

But, again, let me emphasize that balance is important. The time we spend with our spouse needs to take priority over the time we spend with our friends. Willard Harley says, "When you do things separately, you have a tendency to grow apart, each experiencing your most enjoyable moments of fun and relaxation without the other. Couples with separate recreational interests miss a golden opportunity. They often spend their most enjoyable moments in the company of someone else. It stands to reason that the person with whom you share the most

> *"The World needs fewer man-made goods and more God-made men and women."*
>
> —Sarah Anne Jepson

enjoyable moments will give you the greatest dividends."[19] What do these words say to you? Do they help you answer the question raised earlier: "What went wrong along the way?" Maybe as you and your husband have made choices about how to use your time, you've dropped some activities that you could be sharing. We can't say yes to everything, but, per one of the Barnes' favorite mottoes, we need to "say no to good things and save our yeses for the best." Wouldn't it be more beneficial to your marriage to find some recreational activities you can share?

An Attractive Spouse

Men value sexual fulfillment, recreational companionship, and an attractive spouse. And what is attractive? The Bible offers this answer: "Don't be concerned about the outward beauty that depends on jewelry, or beautiful clothes, or hair arrangement. Be beautiful inside, in your hearts, with the lasting charm of a gentle and quiet spirit which is so precious to God. That kind of deep beauty was seen in the saintly women of old, who trusted God and fitted in with their husband's plans" (1 Peter 3:3-5 TLB).

Scripture calls women to be godly and to develop an inward beauty, but wise women also work to make themselves pleasing to their husband's eye—and that's right on target. Now, as a woman, you might not feel that the externals are very important, but doesn't looking nice make you feel better about yourself? Furthermore, externals are important because men are sexually aroused by visual stimulation. When Emilie looks good, I look at her often and I like what I see. When men aren't proud of what they see in their wives, they become more vulnerable to having an affair. A pleasing appearance will invite your husband to touch and hold you—and no one else. Besides, your husband wants to be proud that you're by his side whether at home or in public.

When I was a young boy, my mother wore current fashions and popular colors even though we were a lower-middle-class family. (You don't have to have a lot of money to look attractive!) When Dad came home, she always looked fashionable. She never left home with curlers in her hair or a bandanna wrapped around her head. (She didn't want to embarrass herself if she ran into friends.) Today, Mom is 82 years old and still outwardly attractive. And, funny thing, I married a woman just like mom. Emilie has always presented herself well. When we go out together, I'm proud to introduce her to my friends. (In fact, many companies today interview the wife right along with the husband when he applies for a top management job. The business community knows how great an asset a wife can be to her husband and, rightly or wrongly, bases that judgment greatly on appearance.)

Every married woman needs to ask herself, "Am I looking my best when I am with my husband? Is he proud of my personal appearance?" If you feel you could make yourself more appealing and attractive, know that the resources available are many, ranging from self-help books, friends who will give suggestions, color and wardrobe seminars, and department store consultants who will assist you in developing a new you. And you might follow the example of a friend of ours . . .

Our friend has a specific plan of action to get ready for her husband's arrival home. Each day at 4:00 P.M., she takes a shower or bath, powders and perfumes, combs her hair, and dresses informally. She lives according to another Barnes motto: "A husband should be sad when he leaves for work in the morning, and a wife should be glad to see him come home in the evening." When her husband arrives, her appearance shows that she has been waiting for him and that she cares that he has returned. I encourage you to pay attention to how you look for your husband. You, your husband, and your marriage will definitely benefit!

Domestic Support

What do men value besides sexual fulfillment, recreational companionship, and an attractive spouse? Next on the list is support on the home front. I know that from experience, and I know that from the mail Emilie receives, specifically from the letters from men whose wives make great improvements in their homemaking and organizational skills after attending one of our seminars. What happens in those three hours that changes a wife? The secret isn't a little pill or a magic word. Instead, Emilie offers a biblical perspective on being a wife and homemaker, holds out the hope that women can indeed change the way their homes are functioning, and shares ideas about how to lighten the load and even make homemaking fun. That kind of message is important because men need to know that their wives can handle their households and children in an organized and efficient way, The stereotypical male fantasy of coming home to a well-cooked meal, cooperative and well-behaved children, and a kiss at the door is not too far off what we men really want!

Most of those who aren't at home, longing to get away, are away, longing to get home.

Why is an organized, smoothly functioning home important to a man? One reason is that we need a place to unwind after a day at work. We can feel drained after solving the problems, dealing with the challenges, and feeling the stresses of the day. We need to have a moment of quiet after work. When I arrived home, I used to always say to Emilie, "You think I'm home, but I just sent my body ahead of me!" In reality, I wouldn't be home for another 30 minutes. During that half-hour I regrouped. I didn't handle any emergencies or deal with any bad news. I'd often get a cold drink, sit in my favorite chair, and even take a brief nap. That time allowed me to change gears. After that 30 minutes, I was truly home and able to function as a member of the family. I appreciated Emilie giving me this time to adjust, and she was able to do so because the home was functioning smoothly.

But what can be done when both spouses work outside the home? In that situation, the couple needs to come up with a division of labor so that both the wife and the husband have their needs met. This division of labor often happens rather easily when a couple is first married. Then there is a lot of give-and-take because the husband is accustomed to taking care of himself in some fashion, and he usually continues along fine until the children arrive. At that point, he may worry about not having enough money, take on another job, and begin to resent helping out at home. Tired from a full day, irritated by freeway traffic, and frustrated with his unappreciative boss, he comes home stressed out. If the wife also works out of the home, she has identical stresses and pressures. Such a situation can take a serious toll on a marriage relationship. But you already know that. You want answers!

A solution may come when a couple looks closely at how they are currently using their time and energy around the house. This exercise is easier when the household responsibilities are divided into four categories:[20]

1. *Income-generating activities*. Work that earns money for family living expenses falls into this category. (Does not include volunteer work.)
2. *Childcare*. All tasks dealing with feeding, dressing, supervising, and caring for your children.
3. *Household responsibilities*. Includes cooking, cleaning, washing, ironing, shopping, and organizing the home.
4. *Repair and maintenance of the home, automobile, and mechanical possessions*. Includes mowing the lawn, painting the house, repairing the car, and fixing broken toys.

Using these four categories, develop a work inventory list. What do you and your husband do in each of these areas? List your responsibilities.

Husband	**Wife**
Incoming Generating Activities	
1. Account executive	1. Salesclerk
2. Financial consultant	

Child-care

1. Entertaining children	1. Entertaining children
	2. Feeding children
	3. Dressing children
	4. Bathing children

Household Responsibilities

1. Taking out trash	1. Cleaning house
2. Washing dishes	2. Washing clothes
	3. Washing dishes
	4. Cooking meals

Repair and Maintenance

1. Washing the car	1. Repairing misc. items
2. Mowing the lawn	
3. Repairing the car	
4. Repairing the house	
5. Repairing other items	

The next step is to exchange lists and estimate the amount of time each of your spouse's responsibilities demands from him/her each week: How many hours does your husband spend working as a financial consultant, mowing the lawn, and washing dishes each week? Have your husband estimate how many hours you spend bathing the children, cleaning the house, and cooking meals. Write the number of hours each activity takes each week (15:00, .25, 1.75) and total the numbers. (You both may be surprised by what these totals indicate!)

Next, exchange lists again and review the numbers to see if they fairly represent the time you each actually spend on the activities. Make any necessary adjustments. Then switch again. Working with your spouse's list, write how much time you would like your spouse to spend on each activity: Would you like him to be spending more time entertaining the children and less time working in the yard? Would he like you to spend less time cleaning the house and more time being with the children? With this give-and-take, you and your husband are arriving at a total number of hours that is equitable for both of you. With some serious discussion, the art of compromise, and some adjustments, you'll be able to come up with a workable and equitable division of labor for your family and home.

Our son Brad announced to his wife one evening that on Mondays he was going to be responsible for the evening meal. He may make it, buy it, take the family out, or set up a picnic. Brad was going to relieve Maria of at least one night of dinner preparation. Maria was very excited that Brad sensed that she needed some relief in this area of their home.

One last comment. Couples face very real challenges when it comes to managing a home and raising a family when both husband and wife work outside the home. In fact, many women are deciding to stop working outside the home to become full-time homemakers and mothers. They are realizing that's the only way they can have the kind of home—and children!—they want. And being at home allows that home to be the castle a man wants and a haven of quietness, tranquillity, love, and acceptance that every family member needs.

Admiration

Men need sexual fulfillment, recreational companionship, an attractive spouse, domestic support, and finally, admiration. People have very fragile identities. Men, especially, will go to great lengths to protect their identities as men. They must come to deeply trust a person before they will share who they really are. These facts make a man a sponge for admiration from his wife.

In all of the healthy marriages I have ever seen, the wife sincerely admires her husband—and she doesn't keep it a secret from him or anyone else!

Acceptance—Adoration—Approval—Appreciation—Admiration. When we husbands receive these things from our wives, we can be confident leaders in the home, capable providers, and the men of God He calls us to be.

Your husband truly needs your admiration and approval, and the Scriptures call you to give that to him: "If you love someone . . . you will always believe in him, always expect the best of him . . ." (1 Corinthians 13:7 TLB). Wives, you need to be a cheerleader for your husband. You need to yell, scream, jump, and clap for the home team. When was the last time you cheered for your husband?

It's important that you let your husband know beyond a shadow of a doubt that he is your superman, hero, and knight in shining armor. You can do this with a phone call or personal note that says, "You are special to me! I love you and I believe in you." Make a love basket for him or plan a surprise weekend for just the two of you. These acts of love release your husband to become all God wants him to be. And this kind of admiration encourages, energizes, and motivates your husband. It also helps him stand strong against the pressures and criticisms that may come from work.

We have all heard that behind every great man is a great woman. A loving, admiring, and godly woman will indeed cause a man to gain greater stature than he would on his own. A wife's encouragement can make her husband a better man.

Admire your husband! Support him in his work and his play! Encourage him in his Christian walk! Shower him with acceptance, adoration, approval, appreciation, and admiration!

Your man wants you, his wife, to be his most enthusiastic fan. He becomes stronger and more confident from your support and encouragement.

"Treat me as I am and that's just where I will stay. Treat me as if I were what I could be and that's what I'll become."

Your Husband's Needs

Meeting your man's needs is easier when you clearly understand what they are. I hope this chapter has given you some insight into your man and motivated you to meet his very real—but not always spoken—needs. He needs sexual fulfillment, recreational companionship, an attractive spouse, domestic support, and your admiration. Meet these and you'll strengthen your husband *and* your marriage. And I can almost guarantee that you'll find your husband more interested in meeting your needs and being more effective in doing so. When a man is treated like a king, he in return will begin to treat you as his queen. The world says that you are to receive first, then you give; the Christian is to give first, then receive. Do the opposite of what the world says and you will be astounded at what begins to happen. Be willing to take the risk.

Expressions of Love

- Ask your husband if he has three or four specific needs that you can work toward satisfying.
- Spend some time discussing each point so you understand exactly what he is saying. List these ideas in your journal. You might even want to recite them back to him to make sure you've written them down correctly.
- Rank these needs by priority.
- On the next day, write down in your journal specifically what you can do to fulfill his suggestions.
- Pray over this "action" list, and ask God to direct your path.
- Begin to implement your ideas. Remember, they don't all have to be done at once. You can spread them out over two or three months.

7

Uniquely Created by God

An unlearned carpenter once said, "There is very little difference between one man and another, what little difference there is, is very important."

—William James

Although the world with its unisex fashions and equal rights movements loudly argues that there are no differences between the sexes; those of us who are married know otherwise! It's evident to Emilie and me (as it should be to every husband and wife) that men and women are different—and those differences are much deeper than the obvious physical ones. What circumstances have caused you to realize just how differently you and your husband think? What situations have brought to the foreground the differences between how you and your husband act? Despite what the world says, men and women are different.

Today's culture invites women to expect men to think and act as they do. In a marriage, these unrealistic expectations can result in disappointment and cries of "What's wrong with our marriage? He doesn't even care!" Are you sure your husband doesn't care? You may simply have come up against the fact that a man will show that he cares differently than a woman shows she cares. How we express our love is just one of the many differences between men and women.

What can a good wife do in the face of these differences? She can acknowledge and accept how her husband is different from her. Such acceptance comes more easily when we remember that God made man and woman different. We also need to be aware that some of the differences are due to our individual strengths and weaknesses. You and your husband each entered into marriage with certain strengths and certain weaknesses.

As a young man, I knew that I wanted a wife who would complement me—who would be strong where I was weak. When I met Emilie, I soon fell in love with her because she possessed certain traits that would complement my weaknesses. And she continues to complement me. When people ask me if I'm threatened by Emilie's writing, speaking engagements, and expertise in time management and home organization, I reply, "No, because I am not in competition with Emilie. We complement each other." Likewise, I encourage you not to be threatened by differences between you and your husband. Instead, let those differences help make you a more complete person.

Too often male-female differences are at the root of marital problems. This friction is due not so much to the fact that men and women are physically, emotionally, psychologically, and culturally different from one another, but from the fact that we don't understand those differences or work to accommodate them in our relationships. In contrast, a marriage grows and thrives when a husband and wife understand and accept that God has designed them to be different and complementary.

It is God's will in every marriage that the couple love each other with an absorbing, spiritual, emotional, and physical attraction that continues to grow throughout their lifetime together.

—Ed Wheat

Physical Differences

The most obvious differences between men and women are physical—but that isn't what causes the most friction in marriage. Nevertheless, understanding that God made men and women different physically is important when two lives are blended into one. Let's look at some of the physical differences between men and women:

- Women live an average of eight years longer than men.
- Men are usually stronger and able to run faster and lift more weight than women.
- Men have XY and XX chromosomes; women have XX chromosomes.
- Men have a greater amount of the hormone testosterone, which increases their tendency toward aggression and physical activity.
- Men lose weight faster than women due to the lower ratio of muscle and fat.
- Men have a higher metabolic rate than women.
- A man's blood gives off more oxygen than a woman's.
- Women have greater endurance than men.
- A woman's capacity to exercise is reduced two percent every 10 years, whereas a man's capacity is reduced 10 percent over the same period.
- Men are often physically aroused by visual stimuli; women are usually aroused by touch, caresses, and affection.
- A man's skin wrinkles later in life than a woman's skin.
- Our brains function differently. The male is more left-hemisphere controlled (logical) and the woman is more right-hemisphere controlled (intuitive, emotional).
- Men and women are anatomically different, for instance the man's pelvis is narrow; the woman's pelvis is broad for childbearing.

Again, these differences do not usually pose significant challenges to the marriage relationship, but they do underscore the fact that God made us, male and female, quite different from one another.

Psychological Differences

Far more significant in a marriage than physical differences are the psychological differences between men and women. It is interesting to note that these differences are rooted in physical differences—in the construction of the brain and the way it works. In *What Every Woman Should Know about Men*, Dr. Joyce Brothers offers the following background information:

> The fetus has what scientists call a "bipotential and undifferentiated brain," which means it can go either way (male or female) depending on the influence of sex hormones. The brain is divided into a left and right hemisphere. The left (the verbal brain) controls language and reading skills. We use it when we balance our checkbook, read a newspaper, sing a song, play bridge, write a letter. . . . The right hemisphere . . . is the center of our spatial abilities. We use it when we consult a road map, thread our way through a maze, work a jigsaw puzzle, design a house plan or plant a garden.[21]

Doreen Kimura elaborates on the differences between the male and female brain in an article in *Psychology Today*:

> Sexual differences in the way the brain is organized suggest different ways of thinking and learning. The male brain is specialized. He uses one side for solving spatial problems, the other side for defining a word or verbalizing a problem. The female brain is not so specialized for some functions such as defining words. A woman's right brain and left brain abilities are duplicated to some extent in each hemisphere and work together to solve problems.[22]

If your husband is anything like me, he has a difficult time doing more than one or two things at a time. You are probably like Emilie and able to work very effectively on three, four, or even five things at a time. Women can shift from right brain to left brain activities very quickly, and many times you rely on both hemispheres at the same time. Not us men! We have to come to a screeching halt in the left brain before we shift to the right brain. Now there is nothing wrong with us men; we're just different from you. That's how God created our brains to work!

This data on right brain and left brain explains several psychological differences between men and women.

- Women can better sense the difference between what people say and what they mean.
- Women are more perceptive than men about the meaning of feelings.
- Men have difficulty understanding women's intuition, often thinking that women are too sensitive.
- Women are more perceptive about people than men are.
- Men and women approach problem-solving differently. Men are more analytical and deal with the problem more objectively. Women are less objective; they personally identify with the problem.
- Women can work on several projects at once. Men want to concentrate on only one thing at a time.[23]

As you review this list, what differences do you encounter most frequently in your marriage? Has this list helped you better understand why certain points of tension exist between you and your husband? Some of the psychological differences you run up against may be based in God-given physical differences. Being educated about these differences will help you both live with them—and with each other!

Cultural Differences

The physical and psychological differences between men and women give rise to several cultural differences, although it is sometimes difficult to determine where the unlearned hormonal differences leave off and the learned cultural differences begin. Let's take a look at marriage, commitment, and success in the business world.

In *Why Men Are the Way They Are*, author Warren Farrell states that men are performers who feel they must have an acceptable level of production to be fulfilled. As a performer, a man is competitive and goal-oriented. As an initiator, he is vulnerable to risk and failure and, as a result, often defensive in his relationships—even with his wife. Long-term relationships are risky for a man because they expose his weaknesses, making him vulnerable to great hurt and possible defeat. Instead of moving closer to his woman, a man will defend himself from hurt and defeat by escaping the relationship. If he doesn't stay, his wife cannot hurt him or prove him to be a failure when it comes to marriage. (Statistics show that men are more apt to leave their marriages than women.) To compensate, if not ensure against failure in his relationships, a man works hard to succeed in business. After all, he rationalizes, if he is successful in the working world, he can buy whatever he needs to raise his sense of identity to a level he can live with, even if he is not successful on the home front. Success at work protects many men from the pain of their failure at home.[24]

A man's pursuit of success in business often produces characteristics that make him unlovable at home. When I was working on my master's degree and trying to get a mobile-home business off the ground, I was not always pleasant to live with (as Emilie and the children will tell you). Emilie thought I should value the things she valued (such as home-life and child-rearing), but I was busy—perhaps too busy at times—making my mark on the world. Emilie didn't always understand my desire for success and approval on the job.

Our culture encourages this drive for success and holds up many other standards for "real" men to achieve. When husbands and wives address the culture's expectations of a man, they can avoid several sources of conflict. Which of the following ideas from today's culture are seeds of conflict in your marriage?

- The man is to be the breadwinner in the family. If his wife works, he feels he is less than a real man.
- Men don't quit until they are carried off the field.
- Being macho is important. A man must be in shape, drive the right car, and belong to the right country club.
- Men must know about "men things": boats, trucks, planes, cars, sports, and so on.
- Men always read masculine magazines and never look at women's magazines.
- A man can perform sexually under any circumstances, on demand, and repeatedly.

These ideas seem based on learned cultural differences rather than hormonal differences, but it's not always easy to determine which is which.

Consider the fact that you are basically relationship-oriented while your husband is task- and success-oriented. (By the way, do you think this is learned or unlearned or a little of both?) When a man comes home after a busy day, he has already accomplished what he feels is really important: He has won the battles at the shop, office, or store and provided for his family. He wants to relax, watch television, and read the paper. His wife, however, has waited all day for him and is excited that he is home. He's ready to kick back, but she's ready to kick into gear! She wants to talk!

And talking is far more important to women than it is to men. As you know, you want your husband to share his deepest feelings and most intimate thoughts as well as the events of his day. You want to hear what he has to say, what he's thinking, and what he's feeling, and you want him to listen to you and try to understand what you're feeling. You want to be more than cleaning lady, cook, nursemaid, and childcare coordinator. You want to share in your man's life. You want a relationship based on communication and intimacy.

In her book *In a Different World*, Carol Gilligan summarizes the tension caused by the male's orientation toward tasks and the female's orientation toward relationships:

> Since masculinity is defined through separation while femininity is defined through attachment, male gender identity is threatened by intimacy while female gender identity is threatened by separation. Thus, males tend to have difficulty with relationships while females tend to have difficulty with individualization.[25]

In the academic world, the question again arises: How much of this task-orientation versus relationship-orientation is due to hormonal differences and how much is due to learned cultural differences? The article "Sexism in Our Schools—Training Girls for Failure?" by Mary Conroy raises questions about learned cultural differences between males and females. What do the following statistics say to you?

Love is not all that simple, it is an art that must be learned. We all can learn to love.

—Unknown

- Girls start school with higher test scores than boys. By the time they take the SAT as juniors in high school, girls trail boys by 57 points.
- In coed colleges, women speak up in class 2.5 times less often than their male classmates.
- After the first year of college, women show sharper drops in self-confidence than men do. The longer women stay in school, the lower their self-confidence falls.
- Women receive fewer than 17 percent of all the doctorates awarded in math and physics.
- A mere 10 percent of all high-school principals are women—a smaller percentage than in the 1950s.
- Only 11 percent of all full professors are women.

In her article, Conroy also presents data showing that teachers interact more with boys at every grade level, and it doesn't matter whether the teacher is male or female. The classroom scales tilt firmly in favor of boys, but not because teachers deliberately exclude girls. Most teachers aren't even aware that they treat boys and girls differently, yet studies clearly show they do. Here's what research reveals:

> *Feedback.* Teachers praise boys far more often than they praise girls. Boys also receive more criticism. The benefits? Boys receive more encouragement and more chances to improve. They also learn how to handle criticism.
>
> *Attention.* Boys call out for teacher attention eight times more often than girls—and boys receive it. When they speak out of turn in discussions, teachers accept the remarks as contributions. When girls do the same, teachers tell them to raise their hands.
>
> *Instruction.* When students need help, teachers give the boys more detailed directions, but actually do the work for the girls. Thus, boys learn to be competent and girls learn to be helpless.
>
> *Literature.* Children's books still portray a lopsided view of the world. In those that have won the prestigious Caldecott Medal, ten boys are pictured for every girl.
>
> *Course Selection.* Schools still discourage girls from taking math, science, computer, and vocational classes, according to the Project on Equal Education Rights of the Legal Defense and Education Fund of the National Organization for Women.
>
> *Remedial Assistance.* Girls don't get special help for learning or behavior disorders until they are older and further behind in school than boys with similar disabilities.[26]

Yes, there are cultural differences in our schools, and these differences create tension between the sexes at a very early age.

Besides the primary cultural differences of task- and relationship-orientation, several other cultural differences between men and women—often framed from childhood—shape our role expectations in marriage:

- Boys are supposed to be big, tough, and active while girls are tiny, sweet, and passive.
- Boys should play with trucks, guns, and trains while girls should choose dolls.
- Mothers are more affectionate with girls than boys. Boys are fussier than girls, and girls sleep better than boys.
- Boys are trained to be independent and girls are trained to be compliant.
- Boys are competitive and girls are cooperative.
- Boys form small groups and gangs. Girls develop one-on-one relationships.
- Boys play softball and tell war stories in the locker room. Girls have tea parties and share personal, intimate conversation.
- Girls pattern themselves after their mothers, but boys don't want to copy feminine traits because they fear they will look like sissies around boys.[27]

Where do you see differences between the male culture and female culture causing tension in your marriage? How can understanding the source of some of the differences between you and your husband help minimize the stress they cause?

Sexual Differences

Our society fosters cultural differences between men and women. God Himself, though, created us physically different, psychologically different, and sexually different. As a young man of 22, I thought that men and women shared that sexual excitement and were very much alike in their approach to love and sex. We men move easily from the Wow! of being attracted to a woman to wanting to be sexual with her. Love comes later. Most women, however, are first attracted to a man—then they move to feelings of love. Wanting to be sexual with him comes later when she can trust him. Both men and women need to be aware of differences like this or we will never have our sexual needs met.

When I married Emilie, I learned firsthand about these differences between men and women. I saw quite clearly that women don't approach love the same way. I quickly realized that what Emilie desired most in marriage was love, not sex. She desired sexual fulfillment, too, but she viewed sex as a byproduct of love. While a man grows in his love for his wife through sexual fulfillment, a woman finds sexual fulfillment when she is sure of her husband's love.

Another difference is that men can usually become sexually aroused by visual or physical stimulation from any woman who is sexually attractive. It is easy for a man to engage in sex outside of love. Women, on the other hand, are generally more emotionally oriented. Though capable of being intensely erotic, a woman usually responds sexually to a man who provides her with security, understanding, tenderness, and compassion. Women who have extramarital affairs tend to do so because they are angry, lonely, insecure, or somehow unfulfilled in their marriage relationship. They receive the understanding or compassion they long for from someone other than their husband.

These differences between men and women came to light early in our marriage, as they undoubtedly did in yours. As a healthy, red-blooded male, my love for Emilie was first physically oriented. I expected that she, like me, was easily aroused sexually and that the sex act was a primary focus for her. But when I realized that she placed more value on love, affection, and romance, I had to slow down and make sure I was meeting those needs for her. When I learned how to assure Emilie of my love for her in nonsexual ways, sexual fulfillment came more easily for both of us.

I summarize this basic male/female difference graphically with the following triangles:

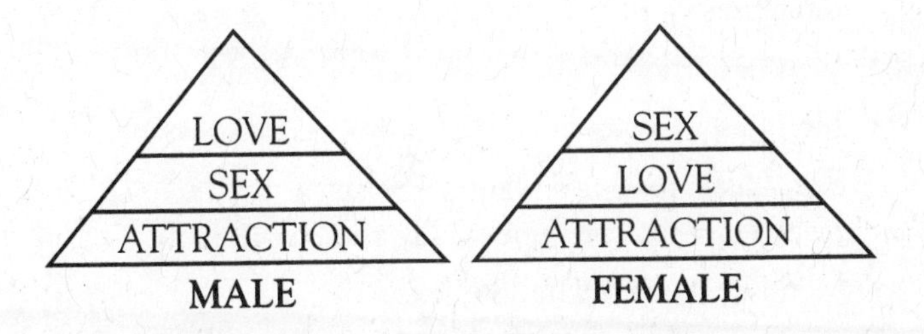

These triangles show that men move easily from being powerfully attracted to a woman to being ready for sex to (perhaps) falling in love. In contrast, most women move slowly from being attracted to a man to falling in love with him to then being ready to share with him sexually. In general, women need to feel in love and loved before they share themselves sexually. We men don't have to experience feelings of love. We have an easier time being ready to share sexually.

Other ways that women differ from men when it comes to sexuality are:

- You love to be romanced with flowers, a note, a box of candy, or suggestions of intimacy.
- You like to be talked to while making love—to be told how your husband is feeling and what he wants. Conversation builds intimacy and excitement for you.
- You like to take your time when being loved, and you take longer than your husband to become fully aroused sexually.
- You need to feel emotionally secure in order to become fully aroused sexually.
- You want your husband to respect your body.
- You need patient and gentle attention as well as verbal appreciation.

Now you probably didn't learn much from that list. Do you know, though, how men differ from women when it comes to sexual fulfillment?

- Men want to know they are doing a good job in life. Any constructive criticism needs to be expressed with love and tenderness.
- Men like women who have a sense of humor.
- Men like to experience the feminine side of women.
- Sex makes men feel wanted. Sex is a way for men to be received or accepted physically and emotionally.
- Men like women who like sex.

What have you learned about your husband from this discussion of sexual differences? How can you stand by him despite the ways he differs from you sexually?

The longer you are married, the more you will see that happiness in marriage doesn't just happen. Always hold hands and tell each other of your love for one another. Never take each other for granted. Learn to love with a willing joy.

Created Differently by God's Design

Men and women, as different as we are from one another physiologically, psychologically, emotionally, and sexually, are made in God's image (Genesis 1:27), and God called this creation good. A Christian husband and wife can be confident that God has put males and females on the earth for a special purpose. To help us bridge our God-given differences, Jesus offers us fundamental guidelines for how to respond to each other. In Matthew 22:37-39, He simply and directly states the greatest commandments in the Scriptures: "You shall love the Lord your God with all your heart, and with all your soul, and with all your mind" and "You shall love your neighbor as yourself."

First, we are to love God, and part of loving God is honoring His creation. You must accept what God has made: unique men and women created for a special purpose. Second, we are to love others, particularly the mate God has given us. Loving your husband doesn't mean changing him—that's the Holy Spirit's role. Loving your husband means understanding how he is different from you and accepting him as he is. I think that one of the lessons of Proverbs 24:3: "By wisdom a house is built, and by understanding it is established," is that a loving understanding for each other as husband and wife establishes your marriage and

---

Grow In Your Faith

A strong faith contributes significantly to successful, happy marriages. A strong bond of shared faith builds a strong bond in marriage.

---

your family. Continuously seeking to understand leads to less anger and frustration in a relationship. You may still be irritated, frustrated, or disturbed by your mate's actions, but at least you will be growing in your knowledge of why he is doing what he is doing.

In Romans 12:2, the apostle Paul offers another scriptural guideline for dealing with differences in our marriages: "Do not be conformed to this world, but be transformed by the renewing of your mind, that you may prove what the will of God is, that which is good and acceptable and perfect." Our culture teaches us to stand up for our individuality and not to give in or accommodate another person's different views or desires—even if that person is our mate. Followers of Christ are to be different. We are to let God transform us "by the renewing of our minds" and so blend the differences between our thoughts and actions that we become truly one.

Our Creator God has created us distinct and very different from one another. When we accept those differences as God-given and even blessed by Him, we will experience the rewards of more positive attitudes, better relationships, mutual respect, and godly character.

Delightfully Different

Emilie and I have experienced the entire gamut of differences discussed in this chapter. We also have learned to see ourselves as delightfully different from one another. Despite different backgrounds and all the physical, emotional, and cultural differences, there has never been an air of competition between us. We have always wanted to complement each other. We are committed to Christ as the foundation of our home and our relationship. I am committed to loving Emilie as Christ loves the church, and she is dedicated to being my helpmate and to reverencing me as her husband. These points of agreement enable us to overcome our differences, and in response to our prayers, God is able to use us to His glory in spite of our individuality.

Early on in our marriage, I was locked into the world's macho-tainted expectations of men. I had tunnel vision regarding the home, children, God, and church. I was typically oriented toward such masculine endeavors as job satisfaction and career goals. I've had to work to move away from a tendency to conform to the world in those areas. Instead of accepting what the world said a man should be, I had to open myself to moving in a godly direction. Romans 12:2 alerted me not to be conformed to the role for a husband that the world defined, but to be transformed to God's definition of marital roles. I realized that if Emilie and I were going to have a healthy marriage and family life, I needed to shatter the worldly mold that threatened our happiness.

As I searched the Scriptures (especially the book of Ephesians), I discovered lessons I've shared with you. I learned that Emilie and I were both made for the purpose of worshiping and enjoying God; that we had each been wonderfully created with unique male or female characteristics; that we weren't to be abrasive to one another in our differences; and that we were, with God's blessing, to complement one another according to His plan. God's Word helped me see marriage afresh and to understand His design for this institution. Every question I had regarding our differences was answered by Scripture. I simply needed to study and apply the truth to my life.

While I was discovering my scriptural role in the home, Emilie was growing too. God was preparing her to share with other women what she was learning about the wife's role in marriage. As each of us came closer to God through studying His Word, we came to know each other better, too. Gradually our differences and inadequacies became less effective instruments in Satan's attempt to weaken our marriage and neutralize our ministry.

Emilie and I had some help along the way, and this help is available to you. First, I highly recommend to you Dr. Tim LaHaye's book *The Spirit-Controlled Temperament* as a tool for you and your husband to work through your differences. Second, the ministry of Fred and Florence Littauer helped us examine our personal strengths and weaknesses and then accentuate the positive and eliminate the negative. Their books also helped us understand that people who are different from us—including our spouses—are not wrong; they're just different.[28] God created each of us to be unique, and our uniqueness adds spice to life as we see things from different points of view.

You have a choice. You can be conformed to this world or transformed to God's point of view. Emilie and I know hundreds of couples who have chosen the latter course. Let God use your differences to lift you to new heights in your relationship.

When Faith Seems Lost

Several months ago, Emilie and I were hosting a radio talk show in Southern California when a lady called in and asked, "How do you love a husband who isn't a Christian?" I thought for a moment then replied, "The same way you would love a husband who *is* a Christian!"

Too often husbands who aren't believers—and even some who are—feel they are in competition with Jesus for the love of their wives. And that is definitely not how to love your husband, whatever his faith! These men often give up on their marriage relationships, believing they can't compete for their wives' devotion against someone as good as Jesus. Wives do indeed need to love God with all their hearts, souls, and minds (Matthew 22:37), but they are also to love their husbands—even when their husbands have hardened their hearts or strayed from the Lord.

The Bible's Commands

God's Word offers very specific instructions to wives about how to love their husbands, but many of these passages are hard for twentieth-century believers to accept. Paul teaches us, however, that "all Scripture is inspired by God and profitable for teaching, for reproof, for correction, for training in righteousness; that the man of God may be adequate, equipped for every good work" (2 Timothy 3:16,17). Consequently, we can't ignore those commands that run counter to our culture and our comfort.

Genesis 3:16 contains two commands: "Then God said to the woman, 'You shall bear children in intense pain and suffering; yet even so, you shall welcome your husband's affections, and *he shall be your master*'" (TLB, emphasis added). These instructions are certainly contrary to what we read in the newspaper, see on television, and watch in today's movies.

Choosing to obey these commands means choosing to love in the ways this book has outlined. It means recognizing and meeting your husband's needs, loving him despite the ways he is different from you, and being his friend. It will mean supporting the decisions he makes, good or bad, even when his heart is hard against the Lord.

Standing by your man when his heart is hard against God is difficult but it may be easier if you understand a few things. First, realize that you are not responsible for your husband's salvation. He is. Second, you are not appointed to be the change-agent in his life. As I've said before, that's the job of the Holy Spirit. Third, your husband's salvation is between God and him.

So what is your role if your husband's heart isn't open to the Lord? Your role is to love him. The Living Bible paraphrases the command of 1 Peter 3:1 this way: "Wives, fit in with your husbands' plans; for then if they refuse to listen when you talk to them about the Lord, they will be won by your respectful, pure behavior. Your godly lives will speak to them better than any words." Let those words encourage you to stand by your man—and recognize that fitting in with his plans won't always be easy!

Several years ago at a Southern California women's retreat, one of the 700 women in attendance came up to me after Fred Littauer and I spoke on this very topic. "Bob," she said, "my husband wants us to sell our home and move to a small town at the base of the Sierra Nevada Mountains on the way to Lake Tahoe. What should I do?" As she shared more details, I saw that her husband wasn't running away and hiding, that he wanted the best for his family, and that he had thoroughly researched the location before planning to start a new business there, so I said, "Go!" The woman said she didn't feel at peace about the move, but I still told her to go. After we had talked for 30 minutes or so, she said she would think about my advice, then she said goodbye.

A year later, at the annual conference, this woman came up to me again. She said, "You won't believe what's happened in the last year! I went home and told my husband that I'd move, and since that day he's been a different man. He gained such confidence knowing that I supported the move. We've purchased a lovely home and joined a wonderful church. The children like their schools, the business is doing better than we expected, and we love it there. Thank you so much for taking the time to share with me your wisdom." She gave me a hug and was on her way through the crowd.

As her story shows, men's hearts *do* soften when they know their wives respect their decisions.

> There are many who want me to tell them of secret ways of becoming perfect and I can only tell them that the sole secret is a hearty love of God, and the only way of attaining that love is by loving. You learn to speak by speaking, to study by studying, to run by running, to work by working; and just so you learn to love God and man by loving. Begin as a mere apprentice and the very power of love will lead you on to become a master of the art.
>
> —St. Francis of Sales

Thirty-Five Years of Prayer

Emilie and I have a dear friend who has also stood by her husband when his heart was hard against the Lord. Emilie met Ruth at church, but they were both also involved in the Christian Women's Association. Ruth was a very proper and elegant lady and the model of hospitality. When you went to her home for dinner or Sunday brunch, you thought you were at a Ritz-Carlton Hotel. Her speech and body language had the polish of a fine finishing school.

Her husband, George, on the other hand, was a self-made oil executive. He had started out working on the oil rigs of Bakersfield and earned his wealth through good investments. His manners were rough, and his speech was punctuated with four-letter words and God's good name.

Ruth and George seemed to be at opposite ends of the spectrum not just in manners but in their relationship to the Lord as well. Ruth shared that she had prayed every day for George's salvation for 34 years, and he didn't seem any closer to knowing the Lord than he had on the day they were married. Emilie and I also began to pray for George, and when it became clear that George enjoyed our company, we invited Ruth and him to our home Bible study. When George said yes, we were all startled beyond belief.

Ruth and George came faithfully every Wednesday night for a year. During that time, George also started going to church, signed up for the men's retreat, and one Sunday morning accepted Jesus as his personal Savior. Ruth had faithfully prayed for 35 years that George would come to know the Lord—and God answered her prayers.

So how do you love a nonbelieving husband? One way is through prayer. Now there are no guarantees about how or when God will answer your prayers, but perhaps you can find hope in the words of preacher Charles Spurgeon: "He who counts the stars and calls them by their names is in no danger of forgetting His own children. He knows [you] as thoroughly as if you were the only creature He ever made or the only saint He ever loved."

Reflections in the Mirror

Once again the issue of respect arises. A hard heart can make respecting your husband as challenging as his bad decisions can. The Bible doesn't offer any escape clauses, though. Paul doesn't list any exceptions in a footnote when he writes the following: "With humility of mind let each of you regard one another as more important than himself" (Philippians 2:3). That is clearly a call to respect!

But respect is a funny thing. When we extend respect to someone, we often receive respect from that person in return. Perhaps even more importantly, as you respect your husband, chances are that he will begin to grow in self-respect. A person who respects himself will, in turn, undoubtedly call forth more respect from you. It's an exciting cycle to begin, and you can play an important role. As Margaret Campolo explains, you can do much to increase your husband's self-respect:

> Remember how much you enjoyed looking terrible in the funny mirrors at amusement parks when you were a child? It was fun because you knew you really did not look like that. You could always find a real mirror and be sure you were you.
>
> In marriage, each partner becomes the mirror for the other. . . . Often a problem in a bad marriage is working like those old amusement park mirrors. A spouse begins to reflect ugly things, and the other one feels that his or her best self isn't there anymore.
>
> Mirrors reflect in simple ways; people are far more complicated. We choose what we reflect, and what we choose has much to do with what the other person becomes. One of the most exciting things about being married is helping your partner become his or her best self by reflecting with love.
>
> Positive reflecting will make your spouse feel good about himself/herself and about you, but it will also change the way you feel. As you look for the positive and overlook the negative, you will become happier about your marriage and the person you married. This will happen even if your spouse does not change at all! . . .
>
> In a difficult marriage, as in the difficult times of a good marriage, ask God for understanding and the ability to do what is humanly impossible. Jesus is our model. And in reflecting our marriage partners positively, we are following His example.[29]

What about your husband are you reflecting back to him? Are you looking for the positive so that he sees his strengths and good points? Do you bring out the best in your husband so that's what he sees when he looks in the mirror of your love? These important questions challenge all of us who are married to look in the mirror we are for our mate.

A Real-Life Example

I will long remember an example of the powerful mirror we can be to one another. Emilie and I were waiting to depart from the airport in Ontario, Canada when I happened to notice two people. From where I was standing, I could see the back of the woman's head and the smiling face of the man she was with. Their hugs and kisses clearly reflected their love and affection for one another. That man certainly loved that woman!

When it was time for us to board the plane, the two people stepped aside to let us go by. Now I had the chance to see the face of this beloved woman. As we passed by, I quickly glanced her way—and was shocked by what I saw. Her face was not the face of a beautiful lady, as I had expected, but that of an accident victim. Her scars, however, did not keep her man from loving her or from showing the world his love for her! He saw beyond the scars to the person she was inside, and his actions communicated his genuine love for her. I don't know whether or not he was a believer, but he was definitely loving this woman as Christ has loved us—unconditionally (John 15:12).

Perhaps your husband's scars, rather than being on the surface, are hidden in his heart. Can you learn from this couple in the airport? Will you offer him unconditional love despite the hardened heart he bears? Listen to the wisdom of Billy Graham's wife, Ruth. She says, "Tell your husband the positive and God the negative." Following this guideline will help you stand by your man with love and respect when his heart is hardened against the Lord and, perhaps, even against you.

The kindest and the happiest pair
Will find occasion to forbear;
And something, every day they live,
To pity, and perhaps forgive.

—William Cowper

Setting the Stage for God to Work

Whatever has scarred and hardened your husband's heart, you are called by God to stand by him. Sometimes that means fervent and faithful prayer. At other times it means acting out a love and respect you may not feel—and then finding yourself beginning to feel those very things! At still other times, supporting your husband may mean biblical and prayerful confrontation by someone who has earned his respect.

Staying with a husband whose heart is hardened will mean calling on God for strength, patience, and hope. God will provide these things. Know, too, that your husband needs you and your prayers. He needs you to love him for exactly who he is right now, not for who you wish he was. *God will enable you to do that.* After all, He is a big God capable of performing big miracles—and you are in an ideal spot to witness Him at work in your marriage.

May God be with you as you learn to appreciate the differences that exist between you and your husband. And may those differences become elements of cement in your relationship, giving new life, spice, and adventure to your marriage. As Emilie and I often say, "Don't compete—complete!"

Expressions of Love

- Tell your husband he is your: superman, shining knight on a white horse, and Mr. Wonderful.
- Have a glamour shot taken of yourself and frame it for him. Get a few wallet sizes for him, too.
- Give him a long, warm hug.
- Tell him you can't wait until he gets home from work.
- Tell your husband you're glad he is there when you reach for him in the middle of the night.

What Makes a Man Feel Loved

8

A Difference in Temperament

Yet those who wait on the Lord will gain new strength;
they will mount up with wings like eagles,
they will run and not be tired,
they will walk and not become weary.
—Isaiah 40:31

Have you ever thought about the fact that men are weird and women are strange? I know that I find Emilie really strange in many areas of her life! For starters, she genuinely likes to clean house, sweep leaves off the sidewalks, iron pillowcases, decorate our home, and play with the grandchildren for hours on end. She also gets quite excited if I don't apply the brakes 100 feet before I get to stand-still traffic. Pretty strange, wouldn't you say?

At the same time, Emilie is well aware that I'm weird. As evidence, she points to the fact that when traveling I won't take the scenic route or stop to go to the restroom because I want to get wherever we're going fast. She also doesn't understand why, when I run an errand, I leave the store with only the one or two items that were on my list.

As if physical, psychological, cultural, and sexual differences weren't challenge enough to overcome in a marriage, most husbands and wives have to deal with yet another critical difference—the difference in temperament. In the preceding chapter, I mentioned how the work of Tim and Beverly LaHaye and Fred and Florence Littauer have helped Emilie and me understand and bridge the gap between our personalities.

Our differences really bothered Emilie and me until we learned about temperaments and recognized how fundamentally different we are from each other. At the same time, we learned the important truth that neither one of us is wrong—we simply differ from one another in temperament and personality. We also learned that a person often marries someone with a temperament opposite his or her own. One reason God gives us such a partner is to provide us with a mate who can be strong where we are weak. But regardless of the good that comes out of temperament differences, the fact remains that dealing with them can be tough.

Before looking closely at temperament issues, it's important to recognize that "different" does not imply superior/inferior, better/worse, or right/wrong. In fact, they can mean strength.

God has created us male and female with distinctive privileges and responsibilities. A wife has been designed to respond to her husband's love, be prepared to help him, and joyfully adapt to his calling in life. According to 1 Peter 3:4, wives are also to possess the beauty of a gentle and quiet spirit as they respect and affirm their husbands—and continue to delight in them all through their lives. This is what your husband needs from you.

The Two Shall Become One

As one of Aesop's fables communicates so well, understanding and accepting temperament differences is well worth the effort. According to the famed storyteller, a wise father sensed disharmony between his sons. He decided to have a conference to discuss this strife. He told each of the four sons to bring a twig to the meeting.

As the young men assembled, the father took each boy's twig and easily snapped it in half. Then, as they watched, he gathered four twigs, tied them together in a bundle, and asked each son to try and break the bundle. Each tried to no avail. The bundle would not snap.

After each son had tried valiantly to break the twigs, the father asked his boys what they had learned from the demonstration. The eldest son said, "If we are individuals, anyone can break us, but if we stick together, no one can harm us." The father said, "You are right. You must always stand together and be strong."

What is true for the four brothers is equally true for a husband and wife. If we don't stand together and let God make us one despite our temperaments, we will easily be defeated. Furthermore, the Bible calls us to such oneness. Genesis 2:24 states, "A man shall leave his father and his mother, and shall cleave to his wife; and they shall become one flesh." God first showed me this verse more than a year before I met Emilie. He had given me a real desire to marry and raise a family, and I knew He was at work preparing me to share my life with a very special woman. At that point, however, I had no idea who that woman would be or what Genesis 2:24 really meant. Those 21 words of this verse tell it all. They sum up the complete teaching on marriage in the Scripture. As I studied that verse, I saw God calling a husband and wife to:

- departure
- permanence
- oneness

Departure

Besides physically leaving their parents' homes, both the husband and wife are to become emotionally and financially independent as well. The marriage relationship—and the new family that has been created—is to be the primary source of emotional health, financial provision, security, and protection.

The bonds of love for one's parents are everlasting, but these connections are to be changed. The new couple will not make an absolute break from their parents, but they must realize that they are now a family and they need to make their own decisions. The new husband and wife must have greater loyalty to each other than to their parents. An early Jewish custom was that the husband was to do nothing the first year except get to know his wife. That's how important total commitment was to the Jewish family. This meant the husband would not go to war, play in a baseball league, teach sabbath school, or go on a fishing trip with the boys. Likewise the new bride was to learn about her new husband. No distractions along the way.

Physically moving from the parents' home is just one kind of necessary departure for a healthy marriage. Husbands and wives also need to depart emotionally. Too many married adults have never consciously stepped away from their parents' emotional control. The process of stepping away emotionally will be gradual, and that process is harder when strong, controlling parents are involved. In that case, the departing young adult may feel guilty about leaving, but such emotional separation is necessary and healthy. It doesn't mean that we no longer care about our parents; it simply means that we are not under parental control. Adults must continue to honor their parents (see Matthew 15:3-9 and I Timothy 5:4-8). The new couple must continually be ready to care for them and to assume responsibility *for* them rather than responsibility *to* them.

Financial independence is another important aspect of leaving home. Leaving financially means we are free to accept financial assistance from our parents, but we no longer depend on them for the funds we need. Again, many adults have not tried to achieve financial independence because they are counting on dad and mom's money to be there for them.

Climb High
Climb Far
Your Goal the Sky
Your Aim the Star

—Anonymous

Achieving independence from one's parents can be a long or short, easy or difficult process. One way to make the separation easier on young people as well as their parents is to follow the example of our Jewish brothers and sisters. In the Jewish wedding ceremonies Emilie and I have attended, parents of both the bride and groom recite vows releasing their children from their authority. Formally releasing one's children could serve to eliminate a lot of uncertainty, guilt, and unhealthy dependence as a new couple works to get established. Again, departure doesn't mean that parents and their married children will never see each other. It does mean a new phase of relationship in which parents regard their children as independent adults capable of managing their own homes, their own emotional lives, and their own financial situations.

As I look at many couples today, I often observe with great sadness that one or both marriage partners have not made the crucial break from mom and dad. You, as a wife, cannot freely give to your husband until you know in your heart that you are more important to him than any other person in his life. Likewise, your husband needs to know that he is the most important person in your life before he can be fully committed to you. We show our spouse that he or she holds that number one spot when, at every level, we leave our parents' house.

Permanence

According to Genesis 2:24, leaving one's father and mother is just the first step toward a strong and godly marriage. Next, the verse states, a man "shall cleave to his wife." The Hebrew word translated "cleave" means "to cling" or "to be glued to" and clearly expresses God's intention that a husband and wife be bonded to one another permanently. Marriage is not an experiment or a trial run. Marriage is a once-and-for-all union. "Cleave" suggests determined action; there is nothing passive about this word.

In light of the fact that marriage should be permanent, God gives these instructions to a newly marriage couple:

> When a man takes a new wife, he shall not go out with the army, nor be charged with any duty; he shall be free at home one year and shall give happiness to his wife whom he has taken (Deuteronomy 24:5).

The Hebrew bridegroom was commanded to set his responsibilities aside for one year and concentrate on making his wife happy. This period of time gave the couple the opportunity to get to know one another and build a foundation for a marriage that would last.

Few newlyweds today have the resources that would allow them to quit their jobs and spend every moment of their first year alone together. But there are some practical steps all married couples can take or apply to reinforce the glue of permanence in their marriage.

Leave your parents' homes and set up a home of your own. If at all possible, do not live in the same house with either of your parents—even if it is more economical to do so.

Spend as much time together as possible. Your marriage is to take priority over nights out with the girls. After all, we can't build relationships with our spouses that will last if we don't spend time together, especially when we're first married. Our spouses are more important than our friends, and our actions need to reflect that fact even if old friends don't understand.

Reserve the bedroom for sleeping and loving—and do this by keeping the television out of your bedroom. Many husbands go to bed to see the end of a movie, the late news, or the last play of the ball game. When this happens, the television robs many couples of the happiness they should be providing each other in the bedroom.

Permanence isn't valued in our culture today, but it's valued by our God, the one who established marriage for us. Furthermore, permanence doesn't happen automatically. It takes work—but the rewards make the work well worth the effort.

Oneness

After calling husbands and wives to leave their fathers and mothers and cleave to one another, God says that the two "shall become one flesh" (Genesis 2:24). In God's sight, we become one at the altar when we say our vows to one another before Him, but, practically speaking, oneness between a husband and wife is a process that happens over a period of time—over their lifetime together.

Becoming one with another person can be a very difficult process. It isn't easy to change from being independent and self-centered to sharing every aspect of your life and self with another person. The difficulty is intensified when you're older and more set in your ways or when the two partners come from very different family, religious, and financial backgrounds. Emilie, for instance, came from an alcoholic family and was raised by a verbally and physically abusive father. I came from a warm, loving family where yelling and screaming simply didn't happen. It took us only a few moments to say our vows and enter into oneness in God's eyes, but we have spent more than 42 years blending our lives and building the oneness we enjoy today. The husband has the primary responsibility to do everything possible to ensure this bonding, to form lifelong ties with his wife. Likewise, the wife is to properly respond to her husband regarding these solidifications. They are to be taken seriously. The following paraphrased Scriptures will help you grasp this concept of cleaving:

You shall cling to the Lord (Deuteronomy 10:20).

You shall hold fast to God's ways (Deuteronomy 11:22).

You shall serve God and cling to Him (Deuteronomy 13:4).

Obey God's voice and hold fast to Him (Deuteronomy 30:20).

Becoming one doesn't mean becoming the same. Oneness means *sharing* the same degree of commitment to the Lord, to the marriage, having the same goals, dreams, and mission in life. The oneness and internal conformity of a marriage relationship comes with the unselfish act of allowing God to shape us into the marriage partner He would have us be. Oneness results when two individuals reflect the same Christ. Such spiritual oneness produces tremendous strength and unity in a marriage and in the family.

Consider what Paul writes to the church at Philippi: "Make my joy complete by being of the same mind, maintaining the same love, united in spirit, intent on one purpose" (Philippians 2:2). This verse has guided me in my roles as husband and father. It has called me, as the family leader, to work to unite my family in purpose, thought, and deed. After many years of trial, error, and endless hours of searching, I can say that we are united in our purpose and direction. If you were to ask Emilie to state our purpose and direction, her answer would match mine: The litmus test for us is Matthew 6:33: "Seek first His kingdom and His righteousness; and all these things shall be added to you." As we have faced decisions through the years, we have asked ourselves, "Are we seeking God's kingdom and His righteousness? Will doing this help us find His kingdom and experience His righteousness? Or are we seeking our own edification or our own satisfaction?" Emilie and I both hold this standard up whenever we have to decide an issue, and that oneness of purpose helps make our marriage work.

The most I can do for a friend is simply to be his friend.

—Henry David Thoreau

Larry Crabb points out another important dimension to the oneness of a husband and wife when he writes:

> The goal of oneness can be almost frightening when we realize that God does not intend [only] that my wife and

> I find our personal needs met in marriage. He also wants our relationship to validate the claims of Christianity to a watching world as an example of the power of Christ's redeeming love to overcome the divisive effects of sin.[30]

The world does not value permanence and oneness in a marriage, and much of our culture works to undermine those characteristics. But knowing what God intends marriage to be, working to leave our parents, cleaving, and becoming one with our spouses, and understanding that our temperament differences can strengthen our unity with our mates—these things will help our marriages shine God's light in a very dark world.

God's pattern is monogamous: Marriage is between one man and one woman. This leaving, cleaving, and oneness results in a new identity in which two people become one. One in mind, heart, body, and spirit (Philippians 2:1,2). This is the pattern for a godly marriage. The blessing of these three principles is to stand before each other naked and not be ashamed (Genesis 2:24,25). Not only in physical nakedness, but also in nakedness of spirit and emotion. We are free from all guilt and shame before our mates. They are to know us as we are known by God—a foundation that will stand the test of time.

Differences in Temperament

It doesn't take this chapter—or the LaHayes' and the Littauers' excellent and thorough work on temperaments—to tell you that your mate is different from you. You are well aware that your spouse doesn't react to situations, people, or life in general the same way you do. The reason is simply that God made your husband different from you. In fact, that difference is undoubtedly part of what made your husband attractive to you in the first place. Now, however, these differences may be a real source of irritation. They may even be affecting your love for each other. But that doesn't have to be the case. Temperament differences can be sources of strength and oneness. Understanding temperament styles can help you bridge the differences and strengthen your marriage.

As Florence Littauer points out in *After Every Wedding Comes a Marriage*, the study of temperament differences goes way back:

> Four hundred years before Christ was born, Hippocrates first presented the concept of the temperaments to the world. As a physician and philosopher, he dealt closely with people and saw that there were extroverts and introverts, optimists and pessimists. He further categorized people according to their body fluids as Sanguine, blood; Choleric, yellow bile; Melancholy, black bile; and Phlegmatic, phlegm. While modern psychologists do not hold to the theory of the fluids, the terms and characteristics are still valid.[31]

While the terms today may vary (colors, animals, "Type A"/"Type B" may be used), psychologists agree that human beings are divided into four basic personality groups: Sanguine, Melancholy, Choleric, and Phlegmatic. The Littauers' Personality Profile (which appears at the end of this chapter and in many of their books) helps readers identify their temperament type and identify their strengths and weaknesses.

At this point, let me add that it is important to look at your weaknesses as well as your strengths. We all proudly look at our strengths, but we aren't nearly as thrilled to look at our weaknesses. Few of us like to confront the negative aspects of our personalities (who likes to hear that they are brassy, interruptive, frank, manipulative, insecure, or moody?), but these negatives can teach us much about ourselves. If our goal is to know ourselves, then we must look into the mirror and acknowledge our negative characteristics. Only then will we be able to decide what to do about those negative traits.

Take some time right now to work through the Personality Profile on pages 129-30.[32] After recording your strengths and weaknesses on the first 40 lines, transfer your answers to the Personality Scoring Sheets on pages 131 and 132 and see how your temperament traits are distributed. You will probably find that most of your traits fall into two categories, although some people will have traits in all four areas. Which two classifications do most of your personality traits fall under?

The two most common combinations are Sanguine–Cholerics: outgoing, optimistic people who make excellent leaders; and Melancholy–Phlegmatics: cautious, introverted folks who like quiet, reflective thinking.

Another standard combination is Melancholy–Choleric, denoting a strong and organized person who accomplishes much and really likes to work. Rather than falling evenly into these categories, 60 percent of your traits may fall into one category and 40 percent into the other. If 60 percent fall under "Choleric," you are probably more optimistic, directive, quick-moving, and able to organize ideas in your head. If 60 percent fall under "Melancholy," you may be somewhat pessimistic, quiet as you give direction, slower to move, and prefer to do your organizing on paper. (A high percentage of business executives are this Melancholy–Choleric combination.)

Like the Melancholy–Choleric personality, the Sanguine–Phlegmatic will tip more in one direction than the other. A mostly Sanguine person will be lighthearted, good-humored, easy-going, fun-loving, and optimistic. If the Phlegmatic prevails, a person will have a dry sense of humor and be quieter, slower-paced, and more laid back, giving the impression that he or she is not concerned about anything. Sanguine–Phlegmatics are always friendly, relaxed, and appealing people, but they can also be poor handlers of money. Also, believing that "all work and no play makes Jack a dull boy," they feel the tug-of-war between the two and may often be unable to get their careers on track.

Florence Littauer's summaries of each one of the temperaments is on pages 133-36.[33] With an open mind and heart, read the two categories into which most of your traits fall. These summaries are not cast in concrete; they merely are an indication of your personality type, a benchmark to help you learn about yourself.

After carefully reading through the two descriptions that your Personality Profile suggested best fit you, spend some time thinking about what you've read. What do these overviews say about yourself? In what areas do you think God would like you to work on becoming more Christlike? Ask your spouse or a trusted friend how accurately the descriptions fit you.

According to 1 Corinthians 11:28, we are to examine ourselves before we receive communion, but such self-examination can be beneficial at other times as well. When we look at ourselves, we can see where God would change us. We can also stop trying to change others and allow them to be themselves. When we allow our spouses to be different from us (and, again, different is not inferior or wrong), our marriages will definitely improve.

God created each of us to be unique. Accept wholeheartedly those areas where your spouse is different from you. Learn from him. Offer your strengths where he is weak, and let his strengths complement your weaknesses. A richer marriage will result!

Expressions of Love

- Make an unexpected date with your husband for lunch during the middle of the week—your treat.
- At dinner talk to your children about your first date with their father.
- Buy him a new shirt and have it specially wrapped. Give it to him as an unbirthday present.
- Give him a coupon for next weekend that says he doesn't have to do any "honey-do" jobs.
- Give him a coupon for a free back rub from you.

PERSONALITY PROFILE

DIRECTIONS: In *each* of the following rows of *four words across,* place an X in front of the *one* word that most often applies to you. Continue through all 40 lines. Be sure each number is marked. If you are not sure which word "most applies," ask a spouse or a friend.

STRENGTHS

1	______	Adventurous	______	Adaptable	______	Animated	______	Analytical
2	______	Persistent	______	Playful	______	Persuasive	______	Peaceful
3	______	Submissive	______	Self-sacrificing	______	Sociable	______	Strong-willed
4	______	Considerate	______	Controlled	______	Competitive	______	Convincing
5	______	Refreshing	______	Respectful	______	Reserved	______	Resourceful
6	______	Satisfied	______	Sensitive	______	Self-reliant	______	Spirited
7	______	Planner	______	Patient	______	Positive	______	Promoter
8	______	Sure	______	Spontaneous	______	Scheduled	______	Shy
9	______	Orderly	______	Obliging	______	Outspoken	______	Optimistic
10	______	Friendly	______	Faithful	______	Funny	______	Forceful
11	______	Daring	______	Delightful	______	Diplomatic	______	Detailed
12	______	Cheerful	______	Consistent	______	Cultured	______	Confident
13	______	Idealistic	______	Independent	______	Inoffensive	______	Inspiring
14	______	Demonstrative	______	Decisive	______	Dry humor	______	Deep
15	______	Mediator	______	Musical	______	Mover	______	Mixes easily
16	______	Thoughtful	______	Tenacious	______	Talker	______	Tolerant
17	______	Listener	______	Loyal	______	Leader	______	Lively
18	______	Contented	______	Chief	______	Chartmaker	______	Cute
19	______	Perfectionist	______	Pleasant	______	Productive	______	Popular
20	______	Bouncy	______	Bold	______	Behaved	______	Balanced

WEAKNESSES

21	______	Blank	______	Bashful	______	Brassy	______	Bossy
22	______	Undisciplined	______	Unsympathetic	______	Unenthusiastic	______	Unforgiving
23	______	Reticent	______	Resentful	______	Resistant	______	Repetitious
24	______	Fussy	______	Fearful	______	Forgetful	______	Frank
25	______	Impatient	______	Insecure	______	Indecisive	______	Interrupts
26	______	Unpopular	______	Uninvolved	______	Unpredictable	______	Unaffectionate
27	______	Headstrong	______	Haphazard	______	Hard-to-please	______	Hesitant
28	______	Plain	______	Pessimistic	______	Proud	______	Permissive
29	______	Angered easily	______	Aimless	______	Argumentative	______	Alienated
30	______	Naive	______	Negative attitude	______	Nervy	______	Nonchalant
31	______	Worrier	______	Withdrawn	______	Workaholic	______	Wants credit
32	______	Too sensitive	______	Tactless	______	Timid	______	Talkative
33	______	Doubtful	______	Disorganized	______	Domineering	______	Depressed
34	______	Inconsistent	______	Introvert	______	Intolerant	______	Indifferent
35	______	Messy	______	Moody	______	Mumbles	______	Manipulative
36	______	Slow	______	Stubborn	______	Show-off	______	Skeptical
37	______	Loner	______	Lord-over	______	Lazy	______	Loud
38	______	Sluggish	______	Suspicious	______	Short-tempered	______	Scatterbrained
39	______	Revengeful	______	Restless	______	Reluctant	______	Rash
40	______	Compromising	______	Critical	______	Crafty	______	Changeable

NOW TRANSFER ALL YOUR X's TO THE CORRESPONDING WORDS ON THE PERSONALITY SCORING SHEET AND ADD UP THE TOTALS.

PERSONALITY SCORING SHEET

STRENGTHS

	SANGUINE POPULAR		CHOLERIC POWERFUL		MELANCHOLY PERFECT		PHLEGMATIC PEACEFUL
1	______	Animated	______	Adventurous	______	Analytical	______	Adaptable
2	______	Playful	______	Persuasive	______	Persistent	______	Peaceful
3	______	Sociable	______	Strong-willed	______	Self-sacrificing	______	Submissive
4	______	Convincing	______	Competitive	______	Considerate	______	Controlled
5	______	Refreshing	______	Resourceful	______	Respectful	______	Reserved
6	______	Spirited	______	Self-reliant	______	Sensitive	______	Satisfied
7	______	Promoter	______	Positive	______	Planner	______	Patient
8	______	Spontaneous	______	Sure	______	Scheduled	______	Shy
9	______	Optimistic	______	Outspoken	______	Orderly	______	Obliging
10	______	Funny	______	Forceful	______	Faithful	______	Friendly
11	______	Delightful	______	Daring	______	Detailed	______	Diplomatic
12	______	Cheerful	______	Confident	______	Cultured	______	Consistent
13	______	Inspiring	______	Independent	______	Idealistic	______	Inoffensive
14	______	Demonstrative	______	Decisive	______	Deep	______	Dry humor
15	______	Mixes easily	______	Mover	______	Musical	______	Mediator
16	______	Talker	______	Tenacious	______	Thoughtful	______	Tolerant
17	______	Lively	______	Leader	______	Loyal	______	Listener
18	______	Cute	______	Chief	______	Chartmaker	______	Contented
19	______	Popular	______	Productive	______	Perfectionist	______	Pleasant
20	______	Bouncy	______	Bold	______	Behaved	______	Balanced
Subtotals	______		______		______		______	

WEAKNESSES

	SANGUINE POPULAR		CHOLERIC POWERFUL		MELANCHOLY PERFECT		PHLEGMATIC PEACEFUL
21	______	Brassy	______	Bossy	______	Bashful	______	Blank
22	______	Undisciplined	______	Unsympathetic	______	Unforgiving	______	Unenthusiastic
23	______	Repetitious	______	Resistant	______	Resentful	______	Reticent
24	______	Forgetful	______	Frank	______	Fussy	______	Fearful
25	______	Interrupts	______	Impatient	______	Insecure	______	Indecisive
26	______	Unpredictable	______	Unaffectionate	______	Unpopular	______	Uninvolved
27	______	Haphazard	______	Headstrong	______	Hard-to-please	______	Hesitant
28	______	Permissive	______	Proud	______	Pessimistic	______	Plain
29	______	Angered easily	______	Argumentative	______	Alienated	______	Aimless
30	______	Naive	______	Nervy	______	Negative attitudes	______	Nonchalant
31	______	Wants credit	______	Workaholic	______	Withdrawn	______	Worrier
32	______	Talkative	______	Tactless	______	Too sensitive	______	Timid
33	______	Disorganized	______	Domineering	______	Depressed	______	Doubtful
34	______	Inconsistent	______	Intolerant	______	Introvert	______	Indifferent
35	______	Messy	______	Manipulative	______	Moody	______	Mumbles
36	______	Show-off	______	Stubborn	______	Skeptical	______	Slow
37	______	Loud	______	Lord-over-others	______	Loner	______	Lazy
38	______	Scatterbrained	______	Short tempered	______	Suspicious	______	Sluggish
39	______	Restless	______	Rash	______	Revengeful	______	Reluctant
40	______	Changeable	______	Crafty	______	Critical	______	Compromising
TOTALS	______		______		______		______	
COMBINED TOTALS	______		______		______		______	

Created by Fred Littauer. Used by Permission.

Popular Sanguine Summary

"Let's do it the fun way."

Desire:	Have fun.
Emotional Needs:	Attention, affection, approval, acceptance.
Key Strengths:	Can talk about anything at any time at any place with or without information. Has a bubbling personality, optimism, sense of humor, storytelling ability, likes people.
Key Weaknesses:	Disorganized, can't remember details or names, exaggerates, not serious about anything, trust others to do the work, too gullible and naive.
Gets Depressed When:	Life is not fun and no one seems to love him.
Is afraid of:	Being unpopular or bored, having to live by the clock or keep a record of money spent.
Likes People Who:	Listen and laugh, praise and approve.
Dislikes People Who:	Criticize, don't respond to his humor, don't think he is cute.
Is Valuable in Work:	For colorful creativity, optimism, light touch, cheering up others, entertaining.
Could Improve If:	He got organized, didn't talk so much, and learned to tell time.
Tends to Marry:	Perfects who are sensitive and serious, but the Populars quickly tire of having to cheer them up all the time, and of being made to feel inadequate and stupid.
Reaction to Stress:	Leave the scene, go shopping, find a fun group, create excuses, blame others.
Recognize by:	Constant talking, loud volume, bright eyes, moving hands, colorful expressions, enthusiasm, ability to mix easily.

Powerful Choleric Summary

"Let's do it my way."

Desire:	Have control.
Emotional Needs:	Sense of obedience, appreciation for accomplishments, credit for ability.
Key Strengths:	Ability to take charge of anything instantly, make quick, correct judgments.
Key Weaknesses:	Too bossy, domineering, autocratic, insensitive, impatient, unwilling to delegate or give credit to others.
Gets Depressed When:	Life is out of control and people won't do things his way.
Is Afraid of:	Losing control of anything, such as losing job, not being promoted, becoming seriously ill, having a rebellious child or unsupportive mate.
Likes People Who:	Are supportive and submissive, see things his way, cooperate quickly, and let them take credit.
Dislikes People Who:	Are lazy and not interested in working constantly, who buck his authority, get independent or aren't loyal.
Is Valuable in Work:	Because he can accomplish more than anyone else in a shorter time and is usually right, but may stir up trouble.
Could Improve If:	He allowed others to make decisions, delegated authority, became more patient, didn't expect everyone to produce as he does.
As a Leader He:	Has a natural feel for being in charge, a quick sense of what will work and a sincere belief in his ability to achieve, but may overwhelm less aggressive people.
Tends to Marry:	Peacefuls who will quietly obey and not buck his authority, but who never accomplish enough or get excited over his projects.
Reaction to Stress:	Tighten control, work harder, exercise more, get rid of offender.
Recognize by:	Fast-moving approach, quick grab for control, self-confidence, restless and overpowering attitude.

Perfect Melancholy Summary

"Let's do it the right way."

Desire:	Have it right.
Emotional Needs:	Sense of stability, space, silence, sensitivity, and support.
Key Strengths:	Ability to organize, set long-range goals, have high standards and ideals, analyze deeply.
Key Weaknesses:	Easily depressed, too much time on preparation, too focused on details, remembers negatives, suspicious of others.
Gets Depressed When:	Life is out of order, standards aren't met and no one seems to care.
Is Afraid of:	No one understanding how he really feels, making a mistake, having to compromise standards.
Likes People Who:	Are serious, intellectual, deep, and will carry on a sensible conversation.
Dislikes People Who:	Are lightweights, forgetful, late, disorganized, superficial, prevaricating, and unpredictable.
Is Valuable in Work:	For sense of details, love of analysis, follow-through, high standards of performance, compassion for the hurting.
Could Improve If:	He didn't take life quite so seriously and didn't insist others be perfectionists.
As a Leader He:	Organizes well, is sensitive to peoples' feelings, has deep creativity, wants quality performance.
Tends to Marry:	Populars for their personalities and social skills, but soon tries to shut them up and get them on a schedule, becoming depressed when they don't respond.
Reaction to Stress:	Withdraws, gets lost in a book, becomes depressed, gives up, recounts the problems.
Recognize by:	Serious, sensitive nature, well-mannered approach, self-deprecating comments, meticulous and well-groomed looks (exceptions are hippy-type intellectuals, musicians, poets, who feel attention to clothes and looks is worldly and detracts from their inner strengths).

Peaceful Phlegmatic Summary

"Let's do it the easy way."

Desire:	Have no conflict, keep peace.
Emotional Needs:	Sense of respect, feeling of worth, understanding, emotional support, harmony.
Key Strengths:	Balance, even disposition, dry sense of humor, pleasing personality.
Key Weaknesses:	Lack of decisiveness, enthusiasm, and energy, has no obvious flaws, and has a hidden will of iron.
Gets Depressed When:	Life is full of conflict, he has to face a personal confrontation, no one wants to help, the buck stops with him.
Is Afraid of:	Having to deal with a major personal problem, being left holding the bag, making major changes.
Likes People Who:	Will make decisions for him, will recognize his strengths, will not ignore him.
Dislikes People Who:	Are too pushy, expect too much of him.
Is Valuable in Work:	Because he cooperates and is a calming influence, keeps peace, mediates between contentious people, objectively solves problems.
Could Improve if:	He sets goals and becomes self-motivated, he were willing to do more and move faster than expected and could face his own problems as well as he handles other people's.
As a Leader He:	Keeps calm, cool, and collected. Doesn't make impulsive decisions, is well-liked and inoffensive, won't cause trouble, but doesn't come up with brilliant new ideas.
Tend to Marry:	Powerfuls because of their strength and decisiveness, but later the Peacefuls get tired of being pushed around and looked down upon.
Reaction to Stress:	Hide from it, watch TV, eat.
Recognize by:	Calm approach, relaxed posture, sitting or leaning when possible.

9

Your Husband, Your Friend

Unless the Lord *builds the house, they labor in vain who build it.*

—Psalm 127:1

Genesis 2:18-25 is a beautiful picture of how God created not only the first woman and wife, but also the first friend. A wife is to be her husband's friend—and that has truly been my experience. Through the years, the love Emilie and I have for each other has grown, and we have become each other's best friend. The Genesis passage suggests that this is exactly what God intends for a married couple. Let's look closely at that section of Scripture.

God gives the woman to the man to be "a helper suitable for him" (2:18). Do you consider yourself a helper or a hindrance to your husband? To his work? To his time at home? Are you "suitable" when it comes to recognizing and meeting his needs? Where could you be more helpful to him? If you're not sure, why not ask him?

God created woman from man's rib (2:21,22). Earlier in Genesis, we learn that God created human beings in His image (1:27). The fact that each one of us is created in God's image calls us to honor and respect one another. Consider for a moment that your husband was made by God in His image, just as you were. How should you treat your spouse? I believe that acknowledging that he has been created in the image of God calls you to respect and honor him and to offer him love and friendship.

Adam perceived Eve as part of his own bone and own flesh (Genesis 2:23). If, like Adam, I rightly understand that Emilie is actually part of me, I will want to treat her as well as I treat myself. I will want to take good care of her and provide for her every need. This kind of husband-love provides a good foundation for the kind of friendship a wife can give her man.

We cannot tell the precise moment when friendship is formed. As in filling a vessel drop by drop, there is at last a drop which makes it run over; so in a series of kindness there is at last one which makes the heart run over.

—SAMUEL JOHNSON

A man is to leave his parents and cleave to his wife (2:24). As we saw in the preceding chapter, the two marriage partners must leave their families and let God make them one. We men help the cleaving happen when we show—not just tell—you, our wives, that you're our most important priority after God. Likewise, a wife needs to let her husband know how important he is to her. Your man cannot be competing with your father or any other male for the number-one position in your life. He must know that you respect, honor, and love him if he is to act out his proper role as man, husband, and father. Besides building up your husband's confidence, your clear communication of your love for him will strengthen the bond of marriage.

The man and the woman stood naked before each other and were not ashamed (2:25). When husbands and wives accept the first four principles—when we understand that we are created in God's image, when we husbands recognize that our wives are bone of our bones, and flesh of our flesh (2:23) and treat her as such, when a wife is a suitable helper to her man, and when spouses cleave to one another—they can indeed stand before one another naked and not ashamed. In fact, that phrase points to a fundamental aspect of true friendship. I don't think a married couple can explore the depths of friendship until they stand before each other open and vulnerable—physically, emotionally, and psychologically. This provides a strong foundation for friendship. Consider the following definition of a friend:

> And what is a friend? Many things. . . . A friend is someone you are comfortable with, someone whose company you prefer. A friend is someone you can count on—not only for support, but for honesty.
>
> A friend is one who believes in you . . . someone with whom you can share your dreams. In fact, a real friend is a person you want to share all of life with—and the sharing doubles the fun.
>
> When you are hurting and you can share your struggle with a friend, it eases the pain. A friend offers you safety and trust. . . . Whatever you say will never be used against you.
>
> A friend will laugh with you, but not at you. . . . A friend will pray with you . . . and for you. My friend is one who hears my cry of pain, who senses my struggle, who shares my lows as well as my highs.[34]

In such a friendship, nothing is hidden. This friendship is built on trust, and the relationship takes time to grow and develop. What better context for this kind of friendship to grow than your marriage? How does your marriage measure up against this description? If you and your husband don't share this kind of friendship, don't wait for him to reach out. Take the initial step and see how he responds. If you have tried before and not been well received, ask God to guide and bless your efforts and then risk reaching out again.

When Pain Is a Roadblock

Perhaps your friendship with your husband is being blocked by some pain that you're dealing with. Perhaps you find yourself in a tunnel of chaos, unable to reach out to him as you'd like. If that's the case, let me encourage you to share your hurt with your husband. But first you may need to address that pain on your own. Don't deny your problem, your feelings, or your questions. Go into that tunnel and feel the pain. In *Honest to God*, Bill Hybels outlines four steps you can take to move from pain and despair to hope and genuine joy.[35]

First, refuse to deny the pain, the frustration, or the heartache you are experiencing. We are deceitful and hypocritical when we deny such feelings. We are not being real when we mindlessly chant "Praise the Lord!" in the face of life's harsh realities. Our parents are imperfect and caused us pain; miscarriages are times for grief; wayward teenagers tear apart their parents' hearts; unemployment brings feelings of fear and anxiety; and sexual abuse results in devastation beyond description. This is only a sampling of the heartache that is in this world, and we need to face realities like these. We need to acknowledge our feelings of fear, loneliness, disappointment, and anger.

Second, honestly tell God how you feel. In the Psalms, David repeatedly—and very openly—speaks of the confusion and pain in his heart: "God, I don't understand this! Why do the righteous suffer while the wicked prosper? Help me understand this!" Often, such authentic outpourings of frustration and anger are necessary steps on the path to wholeness and to a genuine faith in God. If we don't ask these questions, we will simply go through the motions of believing in God and never find an inner confidence in His infinite power or His unconditional love. Share your feelings, whatever they are, with your God who is big enough to deal with them and able to help you handle them.

Third, discuss your pain, disappointment, or heartache with someone else. Galatians 6:2 tells us to "share each other's troubles and problems, and so obey our Lord's command" (TLB). Relief, comfort, and healing come when we share our inner hurts with someone else. The burden somehow seems lighter. Once-overwhelming issues suddenly become manageable when your husband or a friend shows that he or she understands. Often, sharing brings new insight or the suggestion of a course of action you hadn't thought of. Almost always, sharing means less loneliness in your pain.

Fourth, don't hesitate to seek professional help if your unfinished business is weighty and emotionally debilitating. Hybels writes:

> Certainly the healing process requires divine intervention and spiritual growth. And often loving family and friends can provide the human support and wisdom we need. But there are times when competent Christian counselors can provide the necessary blend of spiritual and psychological perspectives. They can help us uncover and understand significant events in our past. And they can help us resolve tensions and initiate more positive relationships with significant people in our lives.

Acknowledging your real feelings and dealing with them can free you to be the kind of friend Christ wants you to be. Without brushing away some cobwebs and first being transparent with ourselves, we'll be limited to a very superficial kind of friendship with anyone else.

Having dealt with your feelings to some degree, make an appointment with your husband. Tell him where you hurt and explain that you truly want to be a friend to him but your pain makes it hard for you right now. If the idea of talking so openly to your husband and letting yourself be so vulnerable is new to you, it undoubtedly sounds frightening. Let me assure you that meeting the challenge will result in greater honesty and intimacy in your marriage. Pray about taking this step and seek counsel. When you're ready, know that God will be with you.

Know too that you are paving the way for a new source of strength for your marriage: genuine and intimate friendship with your husband.

The Rewards of Friendship

You probably don't need to be convinced, but friendship does indeed offer rich rewards. Consider the comments of these people: Upon the death of his friend A.H. Hallam, the poet Tennyson declared, " 'Tis better to have loved and lost than never to have loved at all." Helen Keller once said, "With the death of every friend I love a part of me has been buried, but their contribution to my being of happiness, strength and understanding remains to sustain me in an altered world."[36] Jesus taught that we find ourselves when we lose ourselves (Matthew 10:39).

When have you experienced these truths about friendship? Thank God for those gifts! The value of friendship extends beyond emotional closeness and connectedness. Research, for instance, shows that lonely people live significantly shorter lives than the general population. In his book *The Friendship Factor,* Alan Loy McGinnis points out other benefits of friendship:

> In research at our clinic, my colleague and I have discovered that friendship is the springboard to every other

The Arrow and the Song

I shot an arrow into the air,
It fell to earth, I knew not where;
For, so swiftly it flew, the sight
Could not follow it in its flight.

I breathed a song into the air,
It fell to earth, I knew not where;
For who has sight so keen
and strong,
That it can follow the
flight of song?

Long, long afterward, in an
oak I found the arrow,
still unbroken;
And the song, from
beginning to end,
I found again in the heart
of a friend.

—Henry Wadsworth Longfellow

> love. Friendships spill over onto the other important relationships of life. People with no friends usually have diminished capacity for sustaining any kind of love. They tend to go through a succession of marriages, be estranged from various family members, and have trouble getting along at work. On the other hand, those who learn how to love their friends tend to make long and fulfilling marriages, get along well with the people at work, and enjoy their children.[37]

Whatever you or your husband's past experiences of friendship are, I strongly encourage you to cultivate friendship with your husband. What do you think of when you think of friendship? Intimate sharing? Talking about feelings and hurts and hopes? In contrast, a man's friendships tend to revolve around activities. A friend is someone who goes fishing, plays tennis, or goes to a baseball game with him. Most of a man's friendships grow out of these associations. Shared activities are the point for men, but let me add that Christian men can take male friendships to a deeper level. We can come to a point of real honesty, transparency, and loyalty that makes friendship the source of important accountability and encouragement.

Many men in America are seemingly without friends. They simply don't have (or should that be "make"?) time for friendships. Whether that's due to the structure of their workdays, their personalities, or their priorities, the fact is that men without friends experience a real emotional void in their lives. Also, too often men are in competition with each other. For various reasons, men often experience a degree of distrust and cautiousness around each other. Job titles can also interfere with cultivating a friendship until we come to view one another as God's creation—and even as a mission field of sorts. I've learned that whether men work in a plush office or dig ditches we are all God's creatures, and we all have the same needs. This scriptural perspective has helped me become friends with a variety of men.

The fact seems to stand that women have an easier time with friendships and have experienced different levels of friendship than men do. Our culture, for instance, permits women to be closer to each other than men can be with one another. Women can hug, cry, hold hands, and interlock their arms as they walk down the street, but men are not as free to do these things.

Friendships are another difference between men and women. Men are activity-oriented and women are relationally-oriented. How can you bridge that gap? Simply get interested in your husband's activities. That's one way you can be his friend. After all, "You have to be a friend in order to have a friend."

Five Ways to Deepen Your Friendship

For whatever reasons, it's often not as easy for a man to cultivate a friendship as it is for a woman. Furthermore, if your husband doesn't come from a very demonstrative family, he may not have a good male role model for how to be a friend to his male friends or even to you. You may have to teach him how to be a friend. Following are five points that may help you.

1. *Assign top priority to your friendship*

How important are your friendships? How you spend your time will show you! Each of us does what we want to; nothing gets in the way of our doing what is most important to us. So consider again how important your friendships are to you. Do you say you don't have time for friends—but do you find time to go shopping on a moment's notice? To finish that novel? To catch your favorite television program? If you really want to do something, you'll do it. If you really want to nurture your friendship with your husband, you'll do so. It will take time and effort because good, enduring friendships don't happen instantaneously. The time you invest in your friendship with your husband is time well spent.

One of the hindrances to spending time with your husband may be your kids. They do indeed demand time. But, as Emilie says, "You were a wife to your husband before you were a mother to your children." Your husband needs to be a priority if your marriage is to be strong and your children secure. After all, one of the best gifts you can give your children is to show them that mom and dad are in love with each other.

2. *Cultivate transparency in your relationship*

As we saw at the beginning of this chapter, when we are honest with ourselves about who we are (emotionally and otherwise), we can be a better friend. Our willingness to be open about who we are encourages trust and openness on the part of the other person. So be yourself in your friendships.

Be yourself, first of all, to honor God who made you the unique person you are. Also, discover the freedom that comes with being who you are. When our daughter, Jenny, was in high school, she often stopped by my office. One evening at the dinner table she said, "Dad, you're the same person at work as you are at home!" I considered that a real compliment. That's the way I want it to be. Besides, life is simpler that way. It's not good to wear a lot of masks—you might not remember which face was for which occasion!

> *It is the steady and merciless increase of occupations, the augmented speed at which we are always trying to live, the crowding of each day with more work than it can profitably hold, which has cost us, among other things, the undisturbed enjoyment of friends. Friendship takes time, and we have no time to give it.*
>
> —Agnes Repplier

If you dare to take the initiative and reveal to your husband who you are and what you're feeling, your husband is much more likely to reveal his true self. Nothing will be as effective in drawing him out as your transparency. So take the risk of sharing the joy of your high points and the tears that come at your low points.

3. *Dare to risk talking about your affection*

At our seminars, Emilie and I pass out packages of 64 multicolored cards that say, "I love you because . . . ." We encourage each guest to put these little encouragers in the children's lunch pails, her husbands' attaché case when he leaves on a business trip, in his sack lunch, or with a letter to a friend. The cards can also be used as place cards on the dining room table when guests come to dinner. We encourage the women to take a few moments to complete the sentence: "I love you because . . . you comb your hair each day; you come to the breakfast table with a smile; you work hard to provide for our family; you are only a phone call away when I need you."

People who have used these cards tell us again and again what a good idea they are. I'll long remember the woman who put one card in her husband's sandwich. When he unwrapped his sandwich and took a big bite, he discovered the card but thought his wife had left the wrapper on the cheese! Then he realized he had received a special note from his wife. At first he thought his lunchtime buddies would make fun of him, but one of them said, "I wish my wife would send me a love note!" The wife who had written the note was glad she had risked sharing her affection—and I'm sure her husband was, too. We men do want to know that you love us!

There are lots of other ways you can show us that you care! Consider what I call "the power of the chocolate-chip cookie." When our son, Brad, was about 27 years old and still single, he said that he was looking for a woman who would bake him chocolate-chip cookies. Never had one of his steady dates taken the time to bake him cookies. About two years later, when he was dating the woman who would become his wife, Maria showed her awareness of the power of the cookie. When they were dating, she showed her love by baking Brad chocolate-chip cookies—and she still does so today as his wife.

Our dear friends Bill and Carole Thornburgh also teach a lesson about showing love. In 1987 Bill was diagnosed with leukemia. Eighteen months and three rounds of chemotherapy treatment later, he went to be with our Lord. Soon afterward, Carole was reading a novel where the main character, who was dying of cancer, left a letter for her husband and another for her young children to read when they became adults. Carole desperately wished that Bill had left her a note.

Several days later, when she was getting ready to visit Bill's sister, she decided to take her some of Bill's old books. While going through the books, she found an envelope addressed to her from Bill. He had written her an Easter card two years earlier, and she had tucked it away. Upon rediscovering the card, she was so thankful to God for her husband's written words. At Christmastime 1989, Carole had a precious Easter card from her beloved husband. It read:

A Tearful Week
A Long Week
A Hard Week
A Lonely Week
A Painful Week
A Revealing Week
A Recovering Week
A Reassuring Week
A Peace Week
A Rededication Week
A Friendship Week
A Love Week
A Roller Coaster Week
A Renewal Week
A Glorious Week
A Victorious Week
A Life Changing Week
But A Week I Will Never Lose Sight Of

May God be our source of true love and friendship. You have been so good these days. I love you for it. You have been all a husband would desire. Forgive me, Sweet, for not keeping our love fresh. I love you.

Happy Easter and Happy Beginnings, *Bill*

Bill and Carole spoke openly of their love for one another, and Bill's words offered Carole a sense of his presence after he was gone. I know something about that, too. I have a picture of Bill and me on my desk, and each morning I say "hello" to my friend. He's still my friend even in death.

4. *Learn the language of love*

Each of us needs to learn how to say "I love you." I'm not talking about only speaking aloud those three powerful words (although that's an important thing to do!). We need to also say "I love you" through our respect. Sometimes, for instance, as Emilie is leaving on errands, she will ask if there's anything she can get for me while she's out. Other times she makes my favorite meal—crispy Southern-fried chicken. Or she might hear me say that I'd like a certain new book and—what do you know?—it shows up unexpectedly for no special reason.

I show Emilie that I love her with an evening out, a bunch of fresh flowers, a new blouse, and taking out the trash without being asked. Whenever I choose to show my love this way, I say aloud to Emilie, "Just another way to say, 'I love you!'" Little acts of kindness are powerful and effective ways to strengthen your friendship with your mate. Such acts of thoughtfulness show that you do not take your loved one for granted.

> *Don't flatter yourself that friendship authorizes you to say disagreeable things to your intimates. The nearer you come into relation with a person, the more necessary do tact and courtesy become.*
>
> —Oliver Wendell Holmes

Certain rituals and traditions in our family also enable us to express our love for one another. We kiss each other goodnight and say, "May God bless your sleep." We celebrate our love on anniversaries and birthdays by giving each other small gifts. We telephone one another when we're apart, visit one of our favorite restaurants on special occasions, go out to lunch, attend the theater, and share hugs and corny jokes (my contribution). All of these things—spontaneous acts as well as carefully planned events—make for a special friendship.

One word of caution! Be sure that you are expressing your love in the language—the words *and* the actions—that your spouse will understand! Just because you feel loved when he plans a special dinner out doesn't mean that he feels loved when you do the same! Be a student of your husband. Know what best communicates to him the love you have. Keep your eyes open for common, everyday events that give you the chance to express that love! Our friend Florence Littauer often says, "Be alert to life. Observe what is happening around you."

5. *Give your husband freedom*

As the apostle Paul writes so beautifully in 1 Corinthians 13:4, "Love is very patient and kind, never jealous or envious, never boastful or proud" (TLB). Love is never oppressive or possessive. A wife's unforgiveness and possessiveness can too easily become demands that control her husband. She holds him captive by not giving him the freedom to fail. Maybe she won't let him forget a mistake he made or a hurt he inflicted—despite the command to forgive as we have been forgiven by our heavenly Father (see Colossians 3:13). A wife's words and actions may also discourage her husband and keep him from growing and developing in his spirituality, his work, and even his hobbies. Sometimes men feel suffocated because their wives keep their weekend "honey do" lists so long that they have no time for themselves.

Men fear losing their freedom, and a wife can easily make that fear a painful reality. But let me say that men also need to carefully balance their relationships with the Lord, their wives, and their children, along with their job commitments and recreational activities. They need to be sure they are taking the time to be the husband and father God called them be. Just as husbands are responsible for letting their wives become all God intended, wives are to set their husbands free to be all that God wants them to be.

How can you set your husband free to become the person God would have him be? One key to setting him free is accepting him unconditionally (unless he is violating God's commands). Encourage your husband to be the unique person God created him to be. Be a source of serenity in his life, and grant him the solitude he needs to dream, to recover from life's setbacks, and to be with the Lord.

Also be willing to allow for shifts in your husband's friendship with you. As the seasons of your lives change, you'll notice variations in your friendship. The birth of a child, for instance, means new responsibilities, increased tiredness, an adjustment in the area of sexuality, and, consequently, greater demands on your friendship. Your husband may feel that the child is more important to you than he is. If left unchecked, friendship with your spouse will become strained. After the children leave home, it's crucial that you've maintained your friendship—that you still know each other and like each other. Make sure that, through the years, you don't become business partners held together loosely by your child-raising efforts. The "empty nest" time is the real test of a marital relationship and friendship.

Whatever the season of your life, know that a friendship that is tended, nurtured, and rooted in the Lord will endure. Know too that being your husband's friend will also enable your marriage to endure.

Expressions of Love

- Wink and flirt with your husband at the dinner table.
- "Steal" your husband's car and have it detailed for him.
- Make your husband a hero to your children by giving him a compliment at the dinner table.
- Plan a meal together—have fun cooking even if it's simple.
- Help your husband with one of his dreaded projects.
- Take him on a date and watch one of his favorite movies.

What Makes a Man Feel Loved

10

God Keeps No Records

So then do not be foolish, but understand what the will of the Lord is.
—Ephesians 5:17

One night, after a meeting at church, several of my friends and I were talking about investments. One friend told me about an airline stock that was selling for $23 a share, but was expected to sell for $40 a share within 60 days. I was well aware of my friend's great track record when it came to investing, so his information really got my attention. If I purchased a substantial number of shares at $23 a share and then sold them for $40 a share, I could earn quite a profit! Although I had always preached and practiced, "If it sounds too good to be true, it probably is!" I felt this opportunity was clearly the exception.

The next day I called my stock broker and told him to buy the shares. You wouldn't believe what happened to that company over the next few days. One of its planes crashed in an icy river in Washington, D.C., resulting in the death of many passengers; one of its unions called an all-out strike and shut down the airline; and the chief executive officer left the company and began working for a competitor. And, yes, the stock went down, down, down. When the price hit $13 a share, my friend suggested that I consider buying some more shares to cover my losses and so reduce my price-per-share costs. So again I called my broker and bought more shares, desperately hoping that things would turn around.

I hung onto the stock for another nine months, and the price went down, down, down. At that point, I pridefully decided, "I am not going to sell it now. It will have to come back up in value." A year later, the company filed for bankruptcy and went out of business. My stock was worthless. I lost thousands of dollars, spent a lot of time on the telephone to both my friend and my stockbroker, and worried a great deal about losing all that money. Without exception, this venture into the stock market was the worst decision I ever made.

But despite all the money and time I wasted, Emilie never once reproached me. Not once did she suggest by words or actions that I had failed her. She never once suggested that she thought I was stupid, careless, or shouldn't be trusted with the family money. She stood by me even when I made a series of very poor financial decisions.

Overheard in an Orchard
Said the Robin to the Sparrow:
"I should really like to know
Why these anxious human beings
Rush about and worry so."

Said the Sparrow to the Robin:
"Friend, I think that it must be
That they have no
heavenly Father
Such as cares for you and me."

—Elizabeth Cheney

Respect

Emilie was able to stand by me during my mistakes because she had learned—and was able to live out—two wonderful verses of Scripture. In Ephesians 5:33, Paul writes, "Let the wife see to it that she respect her husband," and in 1 Peter 3:4, the apostle Peter writes, "Let [your beauty] be the hidden person of the heart, with the imperishable quality of a gentle and quiet spirit, which is precious in the sight of God."

In obedience to Scripture and out of her love for me, Emilie continued to respect me when I made poor decisions. She also continued to have that gentle and quiet spirit. When a woman possesses this inner peace and tranquility, she naturally blesses her husband with it. Throughout my financial venture and its aftermath, Emilie's inner tranquility offered me much peace, and her respect for me never faltered. I was never so thankful for a godly wife as I was then.

I encourage you to respect your husband too, whatever the circumstances of your life together. You may be thinking, "I'd respect my husband if he ever did anything worthy of respect!" But God doesn't give us an out when He issues this command. His Word is very straightforward: "Let the wife see to it that she respect her husband" (Ephesians 5:33). Obey God's command to you. Let the grace of His love enable you to respect your mate and extend to him a tranquil and soothing spirit. This touch of God's grace may change your despair over your husband to hope. As God extends His grace to your husband through you, you may also see your husband doing things worthy of respect as he recognizes that you believe in him and will stand with him.

An Escape from Perfectionism

When you consider whether your husband is worthy of your respect, consider what your standards for him are. Are you expecting him to be perfect? Our culture certainly teaches us to demand perfection and be satisfied with nothing less. No mistakes are allowed here! We want everyone and everything to be perfect!

Teachers demanded the right answers. Parents expected us to comb our hair right, brush our teeth properly, and dress appropriately. We learned that we were "bad" when we made poor choices, so now, as adults, we may feel practically immobilized when it comes to making a decision. We don't want to be wrong!

Are you, like our society and perhaps like the family you grew up in, demanding perfection from your husband? Are your demands for perfection based on your fantasy about what a man should be? Or are your demands that your husband be perfect connected to your own pursuit of perfectionism? We cannot find happiness when we are demanding perfection in ourselves or others. But, notes clinical psychologist Marion Woodman, the modern woman is "addicted to perfection, seized by a drive for power and a need to control and dominate."[39] Many of the women in Woodman's study were high-achieving career women suffering from food disorders. Everything in these women's lives had to be perfect—their bodies, their clothing, their work, and their men. The quest for a perfect man has led many women from one man to another. Never satisfied, they look somewhere else for the perfect man, whom Toni Grant calls "the Ghostly Lover."[40]

Are you comparing your husband to a Ghostly Lover? A Ghostly Lover results when a woman idealizes her image of a man. Soap operas, for instance, have contributed greatly to the existence of this Ghostly Lover, the "perfect" male. With their portrayal of love, sex, and marriage, these daytime dramas set up artificial standards which few—if any—real-life men can meet. When a wife holds her husband up against this perfect standard, she will notice the blemishes in her very human spouse, and these blemishes can destroy intimacy. It's one thing for young girls to have fantasies about the special man in their future and to grow up with that fairy-tale prince in mind. But a mature woman lets go of that fantasy and comes to know a real man and loves him for who he is, not who she wishes he were.

It's also hard for many women today to respect their husbands because they find in themselves a sufficient degree of security, strength, and competence. If you have achieved that kind of independence from your husband, what can you do? How can you come to respect your husband more? How can you offer him a quiet and gentle spirit? Only through the grace of God and your submission to Him. God alone can help you

I Need You

I need you in my times of strength and in my weakness;
I need you when you hurt as much as when I hurt.
There is no longer the choice as to what we will share.
We will either share all of life or be fractured persons.
I didn't marry you out of need or to be needed.
We were not driven by instincts or emptiness;
We made a choice to love.
But I think something supernatural happens at the point of marriage commitment (or maybe it's actually natural).
A husband comes into existence; a wife is born.
He is a whole man before and after, but at a point in time he becomes a man who also is a husband;
That is—a man who needs his wife.
She is a whole woman before and after.
But from now on she needs him.
She is herself but now also part of a new unit.
Maybe this is what is meant in saying, "What God hath joined together."
Could it be He really does something special at "I do"?
Your despair is mine even if you don't tell me about it.
But when you do tell, the sharing is easier for me;
And you also can then share from my strength in that weakness.[38]

"not be conformed to this world" and its demands for strong, aggressive, independent women who don't need or respect men. God alone can transform our thinking—men's as well as women's—so that we are not conformed to a world whose message directly conflicts with the Bible's teachings about marriage and relationships.

> *Be not angry that you cannot make others as you wish them to be, since you can not make yourself as you wish to be.*
>
> —Thomas Á Kempis

Demands for perfection—whatever their roots—lead to paralysis, resentment, and a breakdown of love. It is extremely important that you as a wife give your husband the freedom to fail, to be human, to not be perfect. Your husband needs to find that freedom at home because it doesn't exist anywhere else in his world—not at work, not at church, and not even in recreational activities. Let your home be a place where your husband can stop performing and trying to live up to people's standards. Let your home be a place where he can simply be himself. Love your husband for exactly who he is. Believe in him and encourage him.

The Home as a Trauma Center

A home needs to be a place where your husband—as well as you and the children—can be human and fail without fear of judgement or rejection. A home also needs to be a place of refuge when we experience that judgement and rejection from the world. Our home needs to be a trauma center for our healing.

Some time ago, Emilie and I were in the emergency room of our local hospital. A friend of ours had been in a terrible automobile accident, one so severe that the attending paramedics thought that everyone in the car was dead. After quick use of the "Jaws of Life," they took Jimmy to the hospital. In response to a telephone call from his parents, Emilie and I were soon in the emergency room, too. Right away it was clear that the world of the emergency room is much different from anywhere else. It is a place of fear, pain, screams, tears, and life-and-death decisions. In that room of complicated machines, bright lights, and dedicated doctors and nurses, lives are saved and some are lost.

That room is a model of what our homes and our churches should be. Family members and friends alike should enter our homes, knowing they are safe and genuinely loved. Sometimes a home may be the scene of pain and screams and tears, but hopefully those things will lead to healing and renewal.

How can you make your home a trauma center for your husband? Start by being sensitive to how he feels when he arrives home. Listen when your husband needs to unload. Give him a few minutes to unwind by himself if he needs it. Try not to hit him right away with the concerns of your day. Let your home be a place of rest and restoration. Then your husband will be better able to give you what you need to find rest and restoration as well.

I also encourage wives (and husbands) to spend time with the Lord in prayer. Take time to rest in His presence, and you'll discover how He can refresh you. A wife who spends time with her Lord will indeed find the refreshment she needs for herself as well as the refreshment, tranquility, and peace she wants to share with her husband. Emilie made our home such a pleasant place to be that each evening I was anxious to get home as soon as I could. I wanted to be home. It was the best place to be.

Respect Your Man's Abilities

A wife shows her respect for her husband when she supports his decisions, when she is sensitive to what he needs in the home, and when she lets him be the leader in the family. I was reminded how important such leadership is to men when I was a guest speaker at a men's conference in Southern California a few years ago.

In one of our Friday evening groups, the men, who were generally reserved and relaxed in their approach to life, started talking about the fact that they were married to opposites, to women they described as verbal, directed, and take-charge people. They wanted to know how they could be leaders in their own homes. These men wanted to lead, but experience had shown them that their mates didn't want to follow. These men didn't know what to do, and they were confused about what it meant to be the leader in the home.

As I listened to them talk, I saw that these men and their wives didn't have a clear understanding about the difference between work responsibilities and home responsibilities. Several of these men were in business with their wives. They saw that their wives were more competent in certain key areas of the business, and in a few instances, the wife was the president of the company. The wives' strength in the business world caused confusion about the couples' roles at home.

Even one's yesterdays could not continue to stir and move in a man's mind unless there were a future for those yesterdays to make.

— Mary Ellen Chase

I shared with these men that it isn't unmanly to have your wife be more competent in business. I cautioned them not to confuse their leadership in business with leadership in the home and the marriage relationship. Wives and husbands need to look at each other's strengths and determine who will perform which tasks at home. I personally feel that whoever is most competent at a given task should be responsible for that task. If, for example, a wife has stronger business and math skills, why not delegate the family banking to her? If a husband is more skilled or more interested in menu planning, shopping, and cooking, he should feel very comfortable contributing those skills to the family. Such arrangements reflect respect for each person's abilities.

I've seen such arrangements work very well. My brother Ken is a gourmet cook, so he prepares all the family meals. Ken has also been a number-one salesperson in his insurance company and was elected to its hall of fame. Clearly a leader in the business world, Ken is also clearly the leader in his family. His wife, Paula, respects Ken's gifts and so surrenders the kitchen to him. While that may not be the norm, Ken's culinary contributions are the way he uses his strengths to lead. How does the division of labor in your home indicate your awareness of and respect for each other's skills and abilities? In today's marriages, we find that old ways may not always be the best ways to divide up the activities of the home. Each couple must work out their own arrangement that is unique to their situation.

A Look in the Mirror

How your family functions can reveal much about the respect you and your husband have for each other. How you and your husband communicate can also help you take a reading of the level of respect you show one another. A look at two passages will help you look in the mirror.

First, in their book *Choosing to Love*, Jerry and Barbara Cook suggest that wives read the following message to their husbands. Let it be the catalyst for a discussion about your marriage.

> I married a man I respect;
> I have no need to bow and defer.
> I married a man I adore and admire;
> I don't need to be handed a list entitled
> "how to build his ego" or
> "the male need for admiration"
> Love, worship, loyalty, trust—these are inside me;
> They motivate my actions.
> To reduce them to rules destroys my motivation.
> I choose to serve him, to enjoy him.
> We choose to live together and grow together,
> to stretch our capacities for love
> even when it hurts and looks like conflict.
> We choose to learn to know each other
> as real people, as two unique individuals unlike any other two.

Our marriage is a commitment to love;
to belong to each other
to know and understand
to care
to share ourselves, our goals,
interests, desires, needs.
Out of that commitment the actions follow.
Love defines our behavior
and our ways of living together.
And since we fail to meet not only the demands
of standards but also the simple requirements
of love
We are forced to believe in forgiveness . . . and grace.[41]

Now consider a passage from H. Norm Wright's *Quiet Time for Couples*, in which he addresses the issue of respect more specifically. What does this passage show you about your marriage and the respect you show your husband?

> Do you have a respectful marriage? This is part of our calling as believers. Today's passage instructs both husbands and wives to respond to one another with respect. But do you understand what that means? Respect in marriage means ministering to your partner through listening, a loving embrace, a flexible mind and attitude, and a gracious spirit. It means looking past faults and differences and seeing strengths and similarities. It means sharing concerns mutually instead of attempting to carry the load yourself.
>
> Consider the following questions as you evaluate your respect for one another:
>
> - In a tense situation, do I cut off my partner when he or she holds a view different from mine?
> - When I think my partner is wrong, do I become offensive and harsh trying to put him or her in place?
> - In trying to get a point across, am I gently persuasive or opinionated and demanding?

- Am I driven so much by the need to be right that I try to pressure my spouse into my position? Do I intimidate my partner?

Yes, these are questions which meddle. But answering them is a good step toward building a respectful marriage. As one author said, respect begins when we "learn to practice careful listening rather than threatened opposition, honest expression rather than resentment, flexibility rather than rigidity, loving censure rather than harsh coercion, encouragement rather than intimidation."

How's the respect in your marriage relationship?[42]

When we respect our mates in the ways that Norm Wright outlines, we do much to strengthen our marriage. And you, as a wife, have an important opportunity to show your respect for your husband each time he makes a decision, good or bad—and some will be bad. Let me remind you that Babe Ruth struck out more times than any other baseball player—but he also hit 60 home runs in a season and set a new record that no other player has equaled. (Roger Maris did break Ruth's record but with mor games played). Keep in mind, too, that today's baseball players make millions of dollars for batting .300—and batting .300 means getting on base 300 times out of 1000 times at bat. Looked at differently, that statistic means *not* getting on base 700 times—and still the world is willing to pay greatly for a performance like that! So perhaps husbands and

Expressions of Love

- Sign up for a class together at your local college.
- Go outside and watch the sunset together.
- Turn the television off tonight. Listen to some good music, light a fire, and read together.
- Ride along in your husband's golf cart the next time he plays golf.
- Get a babysitter and take your husband out for an ice-cream float.

wives can be a little more forgiving and respectful when their mates make a few bad decisions. When you can do that for your husband, you will be showing him your love in a very powerful way.

You will also be loving your husband with the love of Christ. As Norm Wright observes:

> When we fail, and often we do—God keeps no record of it. God does not deal with us according to our sins (Psalm 103:10), but He accepts us in Christ. Because of the work of Jesus on the cross, you are accepted as blameless. [So] perhaps one of your most important callings in marriage is to follow the model of Christ by being a living benediction to your partner. Help keep your mate from stumbling, and when he or she does fall, don't keep track of it. Scorekeeping isn't a part of marriage; however, forgiveness is.[43]

Answers to prayer often come in unexpected ways. We pray, for instance, for a certain virtue; but God seldom delivers Christian virtues all wrapped in a package and ready for use. Rather he puts us in situations whereby with his help we can develop those virtues. Henry Ward Beecher told of a woman who prayed for patience, and God sent her a poor cook. The best answers to prayer may be the vision and strength to meet a circumstance or to assume a responsibility.[44]

—C.R. Findley

Let go of any unrealistic standards of perfection you have and love your husband for who he is, a fallible human being. Let your home be a place where he isn't constantly evaluated and where he doesn't have to perform in order to be accepted. Focus on his skills and abilities and let him lead from his strengths. Finally, don't keep track of the poor decisions he makes. Your husband will become a more confident decision-maker and a better leader when he knows that you are in his corner no matter what the outcome.

What Makes a Man Feel Loved

11

Made for Work

Then the Lord *God took the man and put him into the garden of Eden to cultivate it and keep it.*

—Genesis 2:15

Fred Lynn, a nine-time All-Star baseball player for the Boston Red Sox, California Angels, Baltimore Orioles, and Detroit Tigers, knows how closely a man's work and his identity are related. Lynn had a career batting average of .283 with four seasons of batting over .300. He had nine seasons in which he hit 20 or more home runs, and his all-time high was 39 home runs in one season. All together he hit 306 home runs. Twice he had 100 or more runs batted in (RBIs) during the season, adding up to a career total of 1,111 RBIs. He won four Golden Glove awards for his defensive play, was the American League's most valuable player as a rookie, and hit the only grand slam home run in All-Star history—and then one day he found himself without a job. The checks of $50,000 to $100,000 he was used to getting twice a month stopped coming in. His response to the situation was something every man can identify with: "When I was playing baseball I knew who I was, but now that I am no longer playing, I don't know who I am."[45]

I can relate to Fred Lynn, and I'm sure your husband can, too. As mysterious as it may seem to you, we men find a great measure of our identity in our work. Whatever a man's job, it can be a source of either great satisfaction or great dissatisfaction—and often, as a man's work goes, so goes his life.

Live for today
Dream for tomorrow
Learn from yesterday
—Unknown

Created to Work

As the Creation passage teaches, human beings were created in the image of God (Genesis 1:26), and one way we reflect God's image is through our work. We were made for work, and we must feel a sense of accomplishment and satisfaction in our work if we are to be content with life in general. And, as many wives have learned from experience, when men are unhappy in their work, family life does not go well.

Sadly, many people—men and women alike—are unhappy in their work. Estimates are that the vast majority of today's working Americans are doing a job that is wrong for them, and my experience in public school administration and the manufacturing industry supports this statistic. One reason for this unhappiness is that people's jobs often don't match their temperaments. I owned a manufacturing business when I first learned about temperament differences and that new understanding helped me see that many of my employees were in the wrong position.

> *Sanguines* need to have fun and be able to talk. If they can't talk or have fun, they'll be restless in their jobs. Sanguines also need to be where their bubbly personalities, optimism, sense of humor, and enjoyment of people work for their—and their employer's—advantage. Sanguines also offer employers creativity,

> the gift of entertaining and cheering up people, and the ability to ease a tense situation. Sanguines make great receptionists, pastors, sales personnel, tour guides, camp leaders, and speakers.
>
> *Cholerics* are born leaders who have the ability to take charge of anything, so they need to have a degree of control in their work. With their innate sense of what will work, they can make quick and usually correct judgments. They also accomplish more than other temperament types in shorter periods of time. Cholerics are team captains in high school, and they eventually become presidents of organizations. They thrive in any position that allows them to lead and therefore make great coaches, military officers, job superintendents, company presidents, and police officers.
>
> *Melancholies* need to have things just right. They organize tasks carefully and analyze them thoroughly. Melancholies set long-range goals, establish high performance standards, pay close attention to detail, and follow through on even the tiniest point, making them effective in accounting, cost analysis, computer-related jobs, and long-range planning. Their compassion for the hurting and those in need make Melancholies good doctors, nurses, and dentists.
>
> *Phlegmatics* want to avoid conflicts and keep the peace at all costs. With their even dispositions, pleasing personalities, and dry sense of humor, Phlegmatics are well liked. Able to stay calm, cool, and collected, they don't make impulsive decisions. Phlegmatics make good fishermen, truck drivers, counselors, workers, mediators, and social workers.[46]

What is your husband's temperament? Does it match his job? If it doesn't, you may have just discovered a key to greater job satisfaction for him and—with your husband more content—a happier home life for everyone.

Two Perspectives on Work

Another key to satisfaction of the job is understanding God's perspective on work and being able to counter the world's view. In the beginning, the Bible teaches, "The LORD God took the man and put him into the garden of Eden to cultivate it and keep it" (Genesis 2:15). God established work as a holy pursuit, and it should be that for those of us who follow Him today. God has ordained work for the human beings He created. We are to work at our jobs and tasks for Him. Ultimately, God is our boss. *He* calls us to work for Him; *He* is the one we serve.

American culture has moved far away from this biblical perspective on work. Today, work is rarely considered a holy pursuit or a means of serving God. Instead, work is what we must do to survive. We live for weekends and reprieves from the time clock and the supervisors. Without goals more noble than earning money to pay the bills, the American work ethic has declined. In their bestseller *Why America Doesn't Work*, Chuck Colson and Jack Eckerd address this decline and show how it is hurting the American family and our future as a nation. As Christians, we have an obligation to take a stand against this declining work ethic and, because we serve the Lord, be the best manager or worker in the company.

The Blessing of Work

Despite what our culture says and despite how we ourselves may sometimes feel, the fact is that work is a holy undertaking. As we've seen in Genesis, God intended us, who are created in His image, to occupy our time with creative and productive efforts that give glory to Him.

> Why would a loving God put His children to work as soon as He created them? Because He knew human labor was a blessing. He knew it would provide them challenges, excitement, adventure, and rewards that nothing else would. He knew that creatures made in His image needed to devote their time to meaningful tasks.

> The writer of Ecclesiastes understood this when he wrote, "Then I realized that it is good and proper for a man to eat and drink, and to find satisfaction in his toilsome labor under the sun during the few days of life God has given him—for this is his lot" (Ecclesiastes 5:18). This writer understood that if we have enough to eat and drink, and if we enjoy our work, we are blessed people.[47]

Think about when you have felt blessed to have enough to eat, enough to drink, and the satisfaction of work you enjoy. Oh, at times the work may be toilsome. The writer of Ecclesiastes acknowledges that fact, and your own experience confirms it. At those times, though, we need to remind ourselves of the privilege it is to serve God in whatever line of work He has placed us.

People often ask Emilie and me if we ever get tired of what we do. We often work very hard in our business, so we get physically tired *from* the work, but we don't get tired *of* the work.

God intends our work to be a natural expression of who we are. Consequently, people who are most satisfied in their job are those whose work is consistent with their natural interests, abilities, and talents. They are doing what they like to do and what they're good at. When our job isn't consistent with who we are, we feel out-of-place, insignificant, and either bored or defeated. When our work matches our interests and calls on us to use our God-given talents, we feel as if we are doing something worthwhile, and we can feel challenged without being overwhelmed. Martin Luther once said, "A man can milk cows to the glory of God."

The beauty of work depends upon the way we meet it, whether we arm ourselves each morning to attack it as an enemy that must be vanquished before night comes—or whether we open our eyes with the sunrise to welcome it as an approaching friend who will keep us delightful company and who will make us feel at evening that the day was well worth its fatigue.

— LUCY LARCOM

Whatever his work, your husband will have days when he feels tired, discouraged, and even overwhelmed. Whatever your husband's work situation and level of contentment, the following suggestions will help you encourage him.

How to Support Your Husband

Understand how important work is to a man. Your husband undoubtedly feels responsible for providing for the family, and that financial responsibility can indeed be a heavy burden. Aside from that practical aspect, work is important because it gives a man a sense of who he is. Men tend to define who they are by what they do. (In contrast, women tend to define who they are by relationships, by their roles as wife and mother.) When work goes badly, men may be rightfully concerned about providing for the family, but they will also experience a threat to their egos and identities that their wives may not understand.

Remember the baseball player Fred Lynn? Unemployment is extremely hard on a man. When my manufactured-housing plant closed down in the recession of 1982, I was without work for the first time in 26 years—and I was lost. I felt I had no identity. I began helping Emilie with her "More Hours in My Day" seminars (it was something to do until I could get a "real" job), but my understanding of who I was remained at a real low point. Oh, yes, I knew I was a child of God, I knew that He loved me, I knew that He cared about me, and I knew that He would provide for me and for my family. I knew all that, but I kept asking, *Who am I?*

One night, when we were doing a seminar in the San Diego area and I was hauling in a load of Emilie's books, tapes, and supplies, a woman met me in the parking lot and wanted to know if I was "Mr. Emilie Barnes." That comment put me two more feet into my grave. I used to introduce Emilie as my wife, and now I am known as Emilie's husband. For 26 years I had been bringing home paychecks, and they were all made out to Bob Barnes. Now all the checks were made out to

Emilie Barnes. What a change! It took me a long time to get over my feelings of inadequacy.

Fortunately, Emilie offered to me what I encourage you to offer to your husband. Emilie remembered and practiced the four A's: acceptance, adoration, approval, and appreciation. She was able to encourage me when my identity was threatened by the change in my work. If you, like Emilie, truly understand how important your husband's work is to him, you are well on your way to having a contented mate. You will also be able to encourage him with the four A's when he hits the rough spots in his work.

Pray for your husband and his work each day. The business climate is brutal, and I can tell you that your husband is continually bombarded with all types of temptations. Your prayers can help him stand strong and true to you and to God. I know that Emilie has prayed for me every day for 42 years. I clearly realize how fortunate and blessed I am to have her stand with me in that way.

Emilie has also stood strong in her faith in God's Word. Together, for instance, we claimed this verse of Scripture, and it strengthened her prayers for me:

> But remember this—the wrong desires that come into your life aren't anything new and different. Many others have faced exactly the same problems before you. And no temptation is irresistible. You can trust God to keep the temptation from becoming so strong that you can't stand up against it, for he has promised this and will do what he says. He will show you how to escape temptation's power so that you can bear up patiently against it (1 Corinthians 10:13 TLB).

There were many times when I knew that Emilie's prayers enabled me to escape temptation's power. I am so thankful that I have a wife who prays diligently for me. Perhaps you can follow her example and pray for your husband. I suggest, too, that in addition to praying for your husband to stand strong against the temptations that arise, you pray for:

- his daily walk with the Lord
- the right kind of friends and associates
- his ability to work in harmony with others
- safety in his travels
- the wisdom to make good decisions
- the knowledge to set right priorities
- contentment in his work
- continuous work
- integrity in the workplace
- your marriage and your children

Be supportive of your husband's work. Men love to have their wives and children interested in what they do, so be enthusiastic about your husband's work. Ask questions and listen to his answers. Read the business section of the newspaper and follow what is going on in his line of work. Keep up with his schedule. Be aware of important clients, meetings, and deadlines. If time, travel, and working conditions permit, visit him at work occasionally and take him out to lunch.

I never did anything worth doing by accident, nor did any of my inventions come by accident; they came by work.

—THOMAS A. EDISON

Children also like to see where dad works and learn about what he does. Besides building a bridge between them and their father, a glimpse into dad's world can help them learn about themselves. One summer, for instance, Brad worked at our plant. He quickly learned that he wanted a college education so that he would have other career options. The motivation to get an education was well worth that summertime experience.

Showing that you are truly interested in your husband's work and getting your children interested in what dad does can strengthen your marriage and your family. Remember too the

Bible's teaching that wives were created to be helpmates to their husbands (Genesis 2:18) and that they are to fit in with their husband's plans (1 Peter 3:1 TLB). Marital disharmony results when husbands and wives disregard these biblical principles. In most successful marriages, the wife readily helps her husband and supports his plans.

Be willing to dream with your husband. Perhaps your husband's dreams are more an irritation to you than a source of shared excitement. Let me offer you a different perspective. Proverbs 29:18 states, "Where there is no vision, the people are unrestrained." In fact, the King James Version says, "Where there is no vision, the people perish." Human beings need to dream. We need a vision to work toward. After all, as the adage says, if you aren't moving forward, you'll slip backward. None of us stay on a plateau for long.

Furthermore, dreams can become goals for the future. I know from my own experience that my dreams for my life—my dreams about the college I would attend, the woman I would marry, the children I would have, the career I would pursue, and the man of God I wanted to become—developed into goals and with God's blessing they have become realities. The first part of reaching my goals involved dreaming about what my life would be like.

Three Things Are Needed

In order that people may be happy in their work, these three things are needed: they must be fit for it; they must not do too much of it; and they must have a sense of success in it—not a doubtful sense, such as needs some testimony of other people for its confirmation, but a sure sense, or rather knowledge, that so much work has been done well, and fruitfully done, whatever the world may say or think about it.

—JOHN RUSKIN

Be willing to let your husband dream and share those dreams with you. We never know when God will bless a dream and bring greater joy and fulfillment than we can imagine. Dreams can help give life direction and motivate you to action. Help your husband dream—and thank God for a man who has a vision for his job, his marriage, and his family.

Be an encourager for your husband. The apostle Paul calls us to "encourage one another and build each other up" (1 Thessalonians 5:11 NIV). The word *encourage* means, literally, "to give courage to another person." Oh, how we men today need courage! Look around at the worlds of politics, business, and even the church. Men need to have courage to stand up for what they believe to be right, and their wives can help them find that courage. With your prayers, your love, and your unwavering support of your husband and his work, you give him the physical, mental, and moral strength he needs to withstand the pressures he faces.

As H. Norman Wright points out, such encouragement "begins with a heart of love and caring, and it is shared through words, attitudes, and actions. Discouraging words cripple, but encouraging words inspire."[48] So choose with wisdom and care the words you speak to your spouse. Be aware of the power of words—power to do good and to do harm. The words that communicate your belief in your husband have the power to do great good. In fact, I believe that your man will never become all he was meant to be until you believe in him and tell him so with sincere words of encouragement. You can share those words through notes sent to his workplace or in a brief telephone call when you know he's going to have a tough day. Consider how you feel when someone offers you words of encouragement. Now give that gift to your husband. Motivate him, support him, and express your appreciation to him. Also be willing to run the risk of a job change if he's not happy in what he's doing. I can't say it too often: *A man gets a sense of identity from his job.* If he doesn't feel significant in his work, he probably won't feel very significant at home. The two go hand-in-hand.

Don't expect to do it all. How can you stand by your husband and his work if you are exhausted by all that you do?

Although the situation is changing, society's call (and, perhaps, especially to women) to try to have it all and do it all and be everything to everyone is still a loud one. Trying to respond to that call puts tremendous strain and pressure on you and your relationships. Individually and as a team, wives and husbands have to say no to many opportunities, requests, and demands. Being able to do so releases them from the bondage of conformity and frees up energy for their relationship and family.

Although Emilie and I teach seminars on time management, home organization, and how to grow a great marriage, we still struggle with a schedule that gets too full, with priorities that get talked about rather than lived out, with goals that seem unreachable, and with expectations about life that aren't being fulfilled. Being involved in a ministry that demands a lot of time and energy, we aren't able to accept all the invitations we receive, entertain guests in our home as often as we'd like, or go away on minivacations for the weekend. We can't do it all—and neither can you. You'll save yourself a lot of time, money, stress, and frustration by not even trying. Attempts to do it all result in damaged relationships, frazzled children, and discouraged parents and spouses.

Even seventeenth-century preacher John Bunyan knew well the problem of trying to do it all and pursuing goals that weren't worth the effort:

Expressions of Love

- Make your husband some popcorn and serve his favorite drink tonight.
- Take an ice-cold glass of ice tea to him while he's working in the yard. He would probably like a cookie or two to go with the drink.
- Play his favorite CD music during dinner this evening.
- Plan his favorite meal. Top it off by renting one of his favorite videos for the evening's entertainment.
- Play his favorite game with him.

Behold how eager our little boy
Is for this butterfly, as if all joy,
All profits, honors, and lasting pleasures,
Were wrapped up in her—or the richest
treasures found in her—
When her all is lighter than a feather . . .
His running through the nettles, thorns and briars
To gratify his boyish fond desires;
His tumbling over molehills to attain
His end, namely his butterfly to gain,
Plainly shows what hazards some men run
To get what will be lost as soon as won.
Men seem, in choice, than children far more wise
Because they run not after butterflies,
When yet, alas, for what are empty toys
They follow them, and act as beardless boys.[49]

What are you and your husband chasing after? Will it stand the test of time? Will reaching your goal make a lasting difference?

> I long to accomplish a great and noble task, but it is my chief duty to accomplish humble tasks as though they were great and noble. The world is moved along, not only by the mighty shoves of its heroes, but also by the aggregate of the tiny pushes of each honest worker.
>
> —Helen Keller

God has called us to enjoy life as a gift—to make the most of every moment and to live with reverence toward God and a keen awareness of the future judgement (Ecclesiastes 2:24; 9:10; 12:13,14). The key to enjoying the gift of life is having a proper attitude toward work. At the end of your lives, neither you nor your husband needs to echo the words of Solomon: "I considered all my activities which my hands had done and the labor which I had exerted, and behold all was vanity and striving after wind and there was no profit under the sun" (Ecclesiastes 2:11). Instead, having regarded your work as the holy pursuit that it is and a higher calling than most of us imagine, you can end your life waiting to hear God's, "Well done, my good and faithful servant."

I encourage you to stand with your husband, believing in him and encouraging him as he milks cows, practices law, works on an assembly line, lectures at the local college, or drives a truck—all to the glory of God!

If I can stop one heart
from breaking,
I shall not live in vain;
If I can ease one life
the aching,
or cool one pain,
Or help one fainting robin
Unto his rest again,
I shall not live in vain.

—EMILY DICKINSON

12

YOUR HERO

The fear of the LORD leads to life, so that one may sleep satisfied, untouched by evil.
— PROVERBS 19:23

As you women know, despite new social freedoms and technological advances that would make your great-grandmother marvel, your life has somehow not gotten any simpler. Have you ever considered how these changes—specifically the social changes—have affected your husband? A new way of life for the American male has definitely emerged since the 80s:

> Little more than a generation ago, life was far simpler for the American male. More often than not, he was family patriarch and breadwinner. His wife catered to his needs and raised his children. His word around the home was law.
>
> Not any more. As a result of the women's revolution and economic pressures, men today face a world in which macho is no longer enough. The new and improved model of male is expected to share in breadwinning and child-rearing and be both tender and tough. Where once

> independence and aloofness was desirable, now openness, sensitivity, and intimacy are prized . . .
>
> Many [men] struggle to blend vestiges of traditional masculinity with what are regarded as softer, or feminine, traits. "Men are confused and searching for their identity," says Mathilda Canter, a psychologist in Phoenix. . . .[50]

In the confusion that arises from the mixed messages we receive from our culture, many men bounce back and forth between being tough and being tender. What does it mean to be a man today? As a wife, you play an important role in shaping your man's image of himself—and you do this by supporting his efforts to be a man of God.

In 1 Corinthians 16:13,14 (NIV), the apostle Paul says, "Be on your guard; stand firm in the faith; be men of courage; be strong. Do everything in love." Paul calls us to develop and maintain a vital relationship with God so we can successfully follow four important guidelines he sets forth for believers:

> *Be on the alert.* We need to be aware of the power of Satan and the temptations he introduces into our lives. Then we will be able to call on God to help us stand strong and be the people He calls us to be.
>
> *Stand firm in the faith.* Our faith in the Lord—our devotion to Him and commitment to serve Him—is to be the source of our strength. Our culture may perceive such faith as foolishness and weakness, but we who believe know that "the foolishness of God is wiser than men, and the weakness of God is stronger than men" (1 Corinthians 1:25).
>
> *Be strong.* We need the support of our spouses as well as the power of the Lord to enable us to stand strong in what we know is right. The demands of the business world can pressure us to compromise our morals. The raising of children calls for integrity as well as a godly strength that gives us patience, wisdom, and love for that important task.

> *Do everything in love.* When we act in love, we can live with strength and sensitivity, toughness and tenderness in the family as well as in the business world. When we submit ourselves first to Christ out of love for Him, we find real power.

As a woman and a wife, you can do much to bring out these virtues in your man. By standing with him and supporting his walk of faith, you encourage your husband to pursue the path God calls him to. You are not to be at war with him. Instead, learn what he needs and how you can be most supportive. Recognize, for instance, that a man will go to great lengths to mask or disguise his true self until he can trust the woman in his life. A man's lack of commitment to a woman is just one way he builds a wall of protection around himself. He doesn't want to be rejected! You can counter this male tendency and ease this male fear by showing yourself trustworthy and clearly expressing your love and support.

Let me remind you that, despite their defense mechanisms, men need love, compassion, and kindness. Sometimes they need that love to be communicated through sex and at other times through spiritual guidance. Sometimes men need mothering, and others times they need a cheerleader. Because your husband's needs are best met in different ways at different times, you must get to know him as well as you know yourself. Does this sound like a lot of work? Let me share another Barnes motto: "Successful people do what unsuccessful people aren't willing to do."

> *God loves each one of us, as if there were only one of us.*
>
> —St. Augustine

I would add here that God will support you in your efforts to know and support the husband He has given you. The writer of Proverbs says: "By wisdom a house is built, and by understanding it is established; and by knowledge the rooms are filled with all precious and pleasant riches" (Proverbs 24:3,4). Ask God to give you wisdom, understanding, and knowledge when dealing with your husband and building your marriage, and know that the rewards and blessings are abundant. Let me offer you the following insights to help you on your way.

Practice Mutual Submission

The social changes I mentioned at the beginning of the chapter have given women new freedom, independence, and power, traits long considered more masculine than feminine. With this new territory have come other traditionally masculine traits like assertiveness, aggressiveness, toughness, and dominance. Many wives today are too masculine in their approach to life, and their behavior certainly doesn't help their husbands understand their role as men.

Consider what Toni Grant has observed about the male-female dynamic in her definitions of a "Good Man" and a "better man":

> A Good man is dependable, committed, considerate, loyal, hard-working, protective, and respected by other men in his field. Most of all, he has courage and integrity. . . . A woman does not choose a Good Man—her hero—in quite the same way she would choose a good lover or playmate. A Good Man, in fact, often does not make a good playmate, and may even at times seem—well—just a little bit boring. Yet this tendency toward predictability is a key sign that the gentleman in question may indeed be a Good Man, a man a woman can count on, a better man than she is.
>
> A better man, quite simply, is a man who has strengths and attributes which the woman can admire and respect, attributes which in some way allow her to yield a certain amount of personal control to him, for she knows that this man—the man she is to view as her hero—is trustworthy and dependable. Without this trust in him, it is impossible to relinquish any control whatsoever, and the woman continues to function in the male role. When with a man she can trust, however, the woman is then able to relax into her femininity, cheerfully relinquish some of her control, and enjoy some of

> the pleasures of being woman. In short, then, a man who is a hero is a trustworthy man to whom a woman feels she can safely surrender and with whom she feels some sense of personal completion.[51]

When you let your husband become a hero to you—when you respect him (Ephesians 5:22,23) and support him—you will see him stand strong in his masculinity. If your husband isn't a hero to you, then you will either find a different hero or become your own hero. Either option will cause distance between you and your husband and weaken your marriage.

As his wife, you stand by your husband by being feminine and by being submissive to him just as, out of reverence to Christ, he is submissive to you (see Ephesians 5:21). When we are submissive to one another, we are free to serve and help each other out of love. Your freely given service and love will help your man be strong in who he is as your husband, as a father, and as a provider.

Recently in Louisville, Kentucky, a woman had watched me assist and encourage Emilie during the conference and commented that I had been a real witness to her. I had indeed submitted to Emilie in terms of the roles we played that weekend, but the thought crossed my mind that in a different situation the roles could have been exactly reversed. After all, Emilie and I are not in competition with one another. In our marriage, Emilie and I have discovered the truth of the Chinese proverb that says, "In submission there is strength." We do indeed find strength when we submit one to another—when we honor and serve each other in every aspect of our lives and try to complement each other. Furthermore, we easily submit to one another because, ultimately, we both live in submission to Jesus Christ.

> *A day spent helping no one but yourself is a day wasted.*
>
> —Abraham Lincoln

Remember that one way to show your love for your husband is by communicating to him your complete acceptance of him. Serving him in love is one way of expressing such acceptance. Remember, too, that we men clearly recognize the difference between being accepted and merely being tolerated! There may be certain things about your husband that you would like to change, but you are not to be the agent of change in his life. Men change—but only when they are motivated to do so. Perhaps rather paradoxically, change comes when we feel accepted just as we are. Consider the following picture of a relationship:

> I love you not only for what you are, but
> for what I am when I am with you.
> I love you not only for what you have made
> of yourself,
> But for what you are making of me.
> I love you because you are helping me to make
> Of the lumber of my life
> Not a tavern, but a temple;
> Out of the words of my everyday
> Not a reproach, but a song.
> I love you for the part of me that you bring out;
> I love you for putting your hand into my
> heaped-up heart
> And passing over all the foolish, weak things
> That you can't help dimly seeing there,
> And for drawing out all the beautiful belongings
> That no one else had looked quite far enough
> to find.[52]

How closely does this poem reflect your marriage? How would mutual submission rooted in a committed love for God help bring about this kind of marital relationship? Mutual submission frees a husband and wife to be the people God calls them to be. It helps you and your spouse, like artists, bring "to the canvas of each other's life the potential that God placed there."[53]

SUPPORT HIM WHEN HE'S LOW

Do you remember Black Monday, October 19, 1987? On that day, the stock market took a sudden and severe nosedive, falling so fast that many sellers could not get out of the market in time to save their investments. Many investors lost thousands of dollars . . . and some lost millions.

One man lost $250,000. How would you react if you watched a quarter of a million dollars disappear before your very eyes? How might your husband react? Would you or he jump off a bridge or turn to alcohol to ease the pain? This particular man did neither because he had learned that his home was a trauma center. He phoned his wife, calmly told her what had happened, and asked her to join him for dinner. They went out to dinner and discussed the day's happenings, just as they had done many times when far less shattering events had occurred. This wife knew how to stand by her man, and her man clearly knew that she was there for him—even at a low point when he was undoubtedly feeling very inadequate in his role as provider for the family. He knew his wife would accept and support him.

In *Women and Sometimes Men*, Florida Scott-Maxwell points out that women often see their husbands' low points and "lesser side":

> One of the poignant paradoxes in the life of a woman is that when a man comes to her, he so often comes to recover his simple humanity and to rest from being at his best. So a woman frequently has to forego his better side, taking it frequently on trust as a matter of hearsay, and she accepts his lesser side as her usual experience of him. . . . She longs to see his greatness but has to meet the claim of his smallness.[54]

Be available to your husband when he comes to you tired, angry, hurt, and moody. Give him the mothering he needs at those times. Trust that his "better side" will again shine through, but in the meantime, follow the example of this investor's wise wife. She had learned to support her husband when he needed her. Even in the face of tremendous loss, she knew how to preserve her husband's dignity and keep him from being overwhelmed by a sense of inadequacy. As a student of her man, she was sensitive to his needs.

We Are Not Alone

We need to feel more to understand others.
We need to love more to be loved back.
We need to cry more to cleanse ourselves.
We need to laugh more to enjoy ourselves.
We need to see more than our own little fantasies.
We need to hear more and listen to the needs of others.
We need to give more and take less.
We need to share more and own less.
We need to look more and realize that we are not so different from one another.
We need to create a world where all can peacefully live the life they choose.

—SUSAN POLIS SCHUTZ

You can use that mysterious intuition God has given you to determine what your husband needs. Remember how you helped him feel supported in earlier hard times, and offer him the same kind of love now. And be sure to pray for your husband when he is struggling. Don't be afraid to share tears with your husband when he's down. Your tears—heartfelt, not phony—may communicate your compassion and love better than any words could. Your tears may also bring out the protectionist and masculine part of your man, and you may see him rise above the circumstances or pain he is dealing with.

At other times, a lighter touch may be appropriate. When we, men as well as women, start taking life or ourselves too seriously, we need an opportunity to laugh. In fact, one of the qualities I like most about Emilie is her ability to laugh; she has a wonderful laugh. Use the gift of laughter carefully, and it will serve you well.

Accepting your husband when he is most needy—whether with sympathetic silence, tears of compassion, or the light touch of some humor—will help him, and your marriage, weather the storms of life.

A Better Dad, a Better Family, a Better Husband

As a man, I can tell you that nothing gives me a sense of my masculinity like being a father to my children—and Emilie did much to help me become a better dad than I would have been on my own. While you are not responsible for developing a good relationship between your husband and your children, you can help him become a better father. Here are a few suggestions.

Give dad a chance to learn to be a good father. Much about the role of a father has changed dramatically since our grandfathers' era. Men now go to childbirth classes and into the delivery room. We carry our newborns, feed them, change their diapers, and, in general, find ourselves very much involved in our children's lives. I encourage you, as a mother, to let this happen in your home.

Despite these positive changes, too many women don't give dads a chance to do more. These moms don't leave the children alone with them. Maybe it's because their ways with the children—their more relaxed approach to a schedule, or even their diapering technique—is different from the moms. The fact is that children need the opportunity to build a relationship with him apart from you, whatever his diapering or cooking skills! Give your children and your husband the chance to be together whether for an evening, a weekend camping trip, a day-long fishing expedition, an afternoon hike, a round of golf, or a set of tennis. Your husband will feel more competent as a father (and, therefore, more sure of his masculinity) when he feels confident about his relationship with the children.

Let dad become his own kind of father. Your husband needs to be free to do things with the children that you, as their mother, won't do. Your choices of activities with the children may be safer, neater, and cleaner than dad's choices—and that is okay. But your children also need to share their dad's kind of fun with him, and that may mean hunting, surfing, sports, roughhousing, skiing, woodworking, or tinkering with the car. At times there will be scratches, torn clothes, stained T-shirts, and smashed fingers, but children will be building a relationship with dad and seeing him model what being a man is all about.

Gordon Dalbey challenges fathers to call their boys out from their mother so that their sons can become men. Dalbey states, "If a boy's manhood has never been confirmed by identifying with the larger community of men through his father, he constantly seeks it with woman after woman, remaining forever 'invalid' in his manhood."[55] It is vital that children—daughters as well as sons—get to know their fathers at play, at work, in church, in all aspects of life. Such interaction also builds up dad!

What is Home?

A roof to keep out the rain. Four walls to keep out the wind. Floors to keep out the cold. Yes, but home is more than that. It is the laugh of a baby, the song of a mother, the strength of a father. Warmth of loving hearts, light from happy eyes, kindness, loyalty, comradeship. Home is the first school and first church for young ones, where they learn what is right, what is good, and what is kind. Where they go for comfort when they are hurt or sick. Where joy is shared and sorrow eased. Where fathers and mothers are respected and loved. Where children are wanted. Where the simplest food is good enough for kings because it is earned. Where money is not so important as loving-kindness. Where even the teakettle sings from happiness. That is home. God bless it.

—Ernestine Schuman-Heink

Make your husband a hero. You've probably heard it said that it's not so much what our children are taught that counts, but what is caught. One important lesson that can be caught by your children is that dad is a hero—and they'll catch that when they see he is your hero.

When I was a high-school student, I caught my dad hugging and kissing my mom at the kitchen sink each evening as she washed the dishes and he dried them. While they cleaned up after dinner, they talked about the day's activities, and, in the process, Dad sent little "love tokens" to Mom. While the hugs and kisses were primarily for the two of them, they showed us boys that Dad loved Mom. What a gift of security that was to us. So when I grew up and started a family, I offered the same love tokens to Emilie, and our children caught us in the act. And—you guessed it—our grown children learned to share love tokens with their spouses in their own kitchens.

Children notice how their parents treat each other, and your children will be well aware of how you treat their father. It is critical that your words and actions are consistent with one another. If you say you love your husband but your actions suggest otherwise, your children will not hear your words. When your actions consistently reflect the love you say you have for you husband, you will be nurturing your children's relationship with their father. When your words *and* your actions indicate your love and respect, your kids will catch it and learn to love and respect their father.

Emilie always did a great job making me a hero to our children. As my biggest fan, she always spoke positively about me even when I wasn't around. I don't remember her ever criticizing me or being anything but completely supportive in front of the kids. (Oh, we had our differences, but we discussed those in private rather than in front of the children.) There are many ways to express your support and love for your husband in front of the kids. Compliment his new shirt, notice his great haircut. Say thank you when he does something for you. Comment on his ability as a golfer or tennis player. Tell him how much you appreciate the fact that he is a good provider.

Acknowledge the long drive he makes on the freeway in order to go to work. Let him know that you value his role as husband and father. In short, make him the hero. Let your children clearly see that you love and respect their father.

When you do this, your husband—as well as the children—relaxes because you remind him that he is significant to the family. You show him that who he is to you and to the children and what he does for the family are very important. His masculinity receives the strengthening it needs.

I remember all too clearly a time when I needed that kind of nurturing. I had a very stressful day and wasn't feeling good about myself. Handing the paycheck over to Emilie, I said, "I think the only reason I exist is to provide a check for this family!" Although caught off-guard by that statement, Emilie was sensitive enough to see that I was struggling with my identity. It wasn't long afterward that she and the children were expressing appreciation for me. They were no longer taking for granted the paycheck or the provider, and I greatly appreciated their reminders that I was important to them.

Your husband is probably a lot like me, so let him know that he is important to you. Be a model for your children so that they can also tell their dad that they love him and appreciate him. As your husband sees himself reflected in the mirror of your love, he will become a stronger leader, a more devoted father, and a more loving husband. With this kind of encouragement, he will have the confidence he needs to be a man of God at home and at work.

Grow Together

As a family that shares a commitment to Christ, spend regular time together doing chores, activities, hobbies, sports, or a weekly game night. Make this a high priority!

Strong and Sensitive

Let me close this discussion of your husband's masculinity with a striking model of a man who was both strong and sensitive, tough and tender. Although this man—a Civil War soldier—lived over 100 years ago, he can teach husbands and wives much about committed love. He models a masculinity that is strengthened by a wife's devotion which, in turn, gives her strength.

July 14, 1861

Camp Clerk, Washington, D.C.

My very dear Sarah:

The indications are very strong that we shall move in a few days—perhaps tomorrow. Lest I should not be able to write again, I feel impelled to write a few lines that may fall under your eye when I shall be no more. . . .

I have no misgivings about, or lack of confidence in the cause in which I am engaged, and my courage does not halt or falter. I know how strongly American Civilization now leans on the triumph of the Government, and how great a debt we owe to those who went before us through the blood and sufferings of the Revolution. And I am willing—perfectly willing—to lay down all my joys in this life, to help maintain this Government, and to pay that debt.

Sarah, my love for you is deathless, it seems to bind me with mighty cables that nothing but Omnipotence could break; and yet my love of Country comes over me like a strong wind and bears me irresistibly on with all these chains to the battlefield.

The memories of the blissful moments I have spent with you come creeping over me, and I feel most gratified to God and to you that I have enjoyed them so long. And hard it is for me to give them up and burn to ashes the hopes of future years, when, God willing, we might still have lived and loved together, and seen our sons grow up to honorable manhood around us. I have, I know, but few and small claims upon Divine Providence, but something whispers to me—perhaps it is the wafted prayer of my little Edgar, that I shall return to my loved ones unharmed. If I do not my dear Sarah, never forget how much I love you, and when my last breath escapes me on the battlefield, it will whisper your name. Forgive my many faults, and the many pains I have caused you. How thoughtless and foolish I have oftentimes been! How gladly would I wash out with my tears every little spot upon your happiness. . . .

But, O Sarah! if the dead can come back to this earth and flit unseen around those they loved, I shall always be near you; in the gladdest days and in the darkest nights . . . *always, always*, and if there be a soft breeze upon your cheek, it shall be my breath, as the cool air fans your throbbing temple, it shall be my spirit passing by. Sarah do not mourn me dead; think I am gone and wait for thee, for we shall meet again.[56]

Major Sullivan Ballou was killed at the first battle of Bull Run, but he had left his wife these few lines of love. She undoubtedly read her beloved husband's words and thought of him whenever a soft breeze touched her cheek. Her husband had been both strong and sensitive, both tough and tender. As his letter reflects, he faced death with courage, standing strong in his convictions and unwavering in his commitment to his country, his wife, and his God. And I would guess that some of his courage resulted from a wife who believed in him, encouraged him, and made him her hero. Sarah had undoubtedly stood by her man's masculinity.

Expressions of Love

- Write with lipstick on your husband's bathroom mirror, "What a hunk of a man; I love you."
- Draw your husband a hot bath with a dab of scented bath oil. Have his robe set out on the bed. Create a romantic atmosphere by having a candle lit in the bathroom. You might even consider joining him after 10 or 15 minutes.
- In a special card, express to your man why he is your hero. Tuck it under his pillow. Be ready for what might happen next!
- Go to bed the same time he does.

Supporting your man's masculinity will indeed encourage him to be the man and husband and father that God wants him to be. Like Sullivan Ballou, who was both tough and tender, your husband can come to know the strength of his masculinity. He can know the balance between strong and sensitive that God intended when He made man. I'm sure God looked down upon Major Ballou and said, "It is good."

You can help your man earn those same words of praise.

Show him in your unique way that he is very special to you and the family. Let your home be a center where he can come home and be small, but while there he can be recharged and become a man of strength. Magnetize him by your attentive behavior and undying support for who he is.

Remember that if you treat a man as he is he will never rise above that, but treat him as he can become and he will rise to that level.

Oh, the comfort, the inexpressible comfort of feeling safe with a person; having neither to weigh thoughts nor measure words, but to pour them all out, just as they are, chaff and grain together, knowing that a faithful hand will take and sift them, keep what is worth keeping, and then, with the breath of kindness, blow the rest away.

—George Eliot

What Makes a
Man Feel
Loved

13

Understanding the Message

Unless the Lord *builds the house,*
they labor in vain who build it.
—Psalm 127:1 (NASB)

There are three partners in a Christian marriage: husband, wife, and Jesus Christ. Proper communication between all three partners is essential for a healthy marriage. A breakdown in dialog between any two members will automatically affect the third member of the partnership. If you and your mate are having difficulty relating, the first area to check is your individual devotional life with God.

Emilie and I have discovered that a breakdown in our communication is usually because one of us is not talking with God on a regular basis. When both of us are communicating with God regularly through prayer and reading His Word, we enjoy excellent communication with each other. The closer you and your husband get to God, the closer you'll grow as a couple.

What is Communication?

"Communication is a process (either verbal or nonverbal) of sharing information with another person in such a way that he understands what you are saying. Talking and listening and understanding are all involved in the process of communication."[57]

Talking

Most of us have little difficulty talking. We are usually willing to give an opinion or offer advice, even when it hasn't been requested. Often our communication problems are not from talking, but from talking too much.

From experience we know that we can say wonderful words in one moment, and in the next say something hurtful or embarrassing. First Peter 3:10 says, "If you want a happy, good life, keep control of your tongue, and guard your lips from telling lies" (TLB). Solomon said: "A word aptly spoken is like apples of gold in settings of silver" (Proverb 25:11 NIV). Teaching on this passage, Florence Littauer says that our words should be like silver boxes tied with bows. I like that description because I can visualize husbands and wives giving verbal gifts to each other in their conversations. In Ephesians 4:29 we're admonished to "let no unwholesome word proceed from [our] mouth[s], but only such a word as is good for edification according to the need of the moment, that it may give grace to those who hear." We are not to speak ugly words that tear down our mates; we are to speak uplifting and encouraging words that will bring a blessing.

I like not only to be loved, but to be told that I am loved; the realm of silence is large enough beyond the grave.

—George Elliot

One of the ways Emilie and I have filled our speech with love is in the careful choice of words we use with each other. We like the two lists Denis Waitley shares in his book *Seeds of*

Greatness. He indicates words we should forget and words we should remember in loving conversation:

Words to Forget	Words to Remember
I can't	I can
I'll try	I will
I have to	I want to
I should have	I will do
I could have	My goal
Someday	Today
If only	Next time
Yes, but	I understand
Problem	Opportunity
Difficult	Challenging
Stressed	Motivated
Worried	Interested
Impossible	Possible
I, me, my	You, your
Hate	Love[58]

Are there some words in your communication you need to forget? Replace them with words that affirm your love and deepen your intimacy. Consciously watch your language. Communicate by using positive, loving words.

Another form of "talking," is through notes of encouragement. Sometimes Emilie and I leave notes for each other in unusual places to lift up one another: in a lunch sack, suitcase, briefcase, or under a pillow. We've even used a water-based felt marker to write messages to each other on the tile inside the shower stall. (After being read, the message can be easily washed off.)

A card or letter sent through the mail seems to be more enthusiastically received than a note left out in plain sight. Sometimes homemade cards are a lot of fun to make and send. Remember—Everybody likes to get good mail!

Listening

Of Wright's three elements of communication: talking, listening, and understanding, listening is usually the trouble area. Instead of patiently hearing what our mates have to say, most of us can hardly wait until they stop talking so we can put in our two cents' worth. We need to discover how we can savor our partners' words like we enjoy a fine meal, a thoughtful gift, lovely music, or a great book. To truly listen is to take time to digest the content of the message and let it get under your skin and into your system. The following questions and discussions will help you probe your personal listening attitudes and habits.

1. Have you already stopped listening?

In some couples, one or both partners have already stopped listening to the other. They block out everything their mates say by hiding behind a newspaper or working long and late hours. If you find yourself shouting at your mate to be heard, you are probably married to someone who has stopped listening.

When your mate stops listening to you, you will probably react by withdrawing, talking less, or overcompensating by talking louder and longer. These reactions aren't productive in the long run. If your mate isn't listening to you, it may be because you are not communicating at a level that invites your mate's participation. In his book *Why Am I Afraid to Tell You Who I Am?* John Powell lists five levels of communication, each one deeper and more meaningful than the last.[59] Try to identify the level you and your mate most commonly employ, then seek to improve your communication by moving to deeper levels.

Level five is cliché conversation, which includes everyday, casual conversation based on safe statements like "How are you?" "How's your family?" "Where have you been?" "I like your suit." Lacking in depth, cliché conversation barely acknowledges that the other person is alive.

Level four is reporting the facts about others. At this level you are quoting others instead of giving personal commentary: "It will be a sunny day." "The Orioles lost their twentieth straight game." "The score of the football game was 17 to 6." There is little or no emotion or commitment at this level.

Level three, sharing your ideas and judgments, is where real communication begins. Here you are willing to step out and risk expressing a personal opinion in order to be part of the decision-making process. You may feel insecure at this level, but at least you are willing to take a chance. People who are threatened at this level often retreat to communication levels four or five.

Level two is your feelings and emotions. At this level you express how you feel about the facts, ideas, and judgments expressed: "I feel so much better when the sun is shining." Information is not enough at this level. Feelings must be shared in order to communicate.

Level one encompasses complete emotional and personal truthful communication. This level of communication requires complete openness and honesty and involves great risk. All deep and enriching relationships operate at this level. It takes a great deal of trust, love, and understanding to communicate truthfully. This level is not a dumping ground, but a place where each partner treats the other with love and concern. In this level, you ask questions such as: "Honey, what seems to be troubling you lately?" "How may I pray for you?" and "What have I done lately to disappoint you?"

Use the following questions to help you evaluate the present communication level in your marriage:

- What level of communication is most common to you and your partner?
- What are the indicators of your communication level?
- What actions can you take to move your communication to a deeper level?

If you as a couple have stopped listening to each other, here are some helpful tips we have learned about listening that you should take to heart:

- Realize that each of you has a basic need to be listened to.
- Listen intently when your partner is talking to you. Don't just think about your own responses. Listening is more than politely waiting your turn to speak.
- Listen objectively. Put down the newspaper, turn off the television, look your partner in the eye, and pay attention.
- Reach out and care about what is being said. Listening is active participation, not passive observance.
- Move past the surface message and get to the heart of what is being said. Listening is more than hearing words.
- Discipline yourself to listen. Listening doesn't come naturally or easily to any of us. Most of us are more comfortable when we are in control and speaking.
- Receive and process the message sent. Try to understand what is being said. At times the message may be painful, but you will be stretched if you continue to listen.

Timing is an important element in the success of communication. Honor your mate by selecting the best times to talk, listen, and understand. Emilie always allows me the first 15 to 30 minutes after I arrive home from work to unwind. We don't bring up difficult topics during that time unless there is an emergency. We reserve mealtimes for pleasant, edifying, and uplifting conversation. Serious topics are saved until after the pangs of hunger have been satisfied. Then, between dinner and bedtime, we cover more serious issues. If it doesn't pertain to the whole family, reserve a time when you and your husband are alone.

If you have a very serious topic to address, you might want to secure a babysitter and invite your mate out to dinner so you can talk away from the distractions at home.

2. *Do you presume or judge as you listen?*

As a father, I can recall many times when our children would come to me asking permission to do something or to go somewhere. Often I would start shaking my head no before they finished asking their questions. This was a great disservice to them because I was telling them their opinions and requests were unimportant before they had time to fully express them. The answer may still have been no, but they would have accepted and understood better if I had listened to their requests, discussed them, and then given my answer.

Just as the lovely flowers lend their sweetness to each day, may we touch the lives of those we meet in a kind and gentle way.

—UNKNOWN

Proverbs 18:13 in the Living Bible says: "What a shame—yes, how stupid!—to decide before knowing the facts!" As a couple, we must thoroughly hear the other person out before giving a response or pronouncing a judgment. Listen to your mate when he begins to talk about a new job, a new home, or a transfer. These are the beginnings of his sharing.

3. *Do you touch when you listen?*

Touching is probably the best way to tell your mate that you are listening. The amount of encouragement and affirmation that can be communicated through touch is astounding. Often no words are needed when there is a hug, a hand clasp, an arm around the shoulder, or even a playful nudge. Sometimes your mate just wants to be held. He is crying out, "Are you listening? Do you care?" Your touch assures him that you are in tune with what he is saying.

4. *Are you a gut-level listener?*

Gut-level listeners are intense listeners. They focus beyond what their mates say to hear what their mates mean. They are open and compassionate, asking in-depth questions and ready to communicate at level one. Without gut-level listening we often miss the real meaning of the words being spoken. We must learn to listen more with our hearts and souls than with our ears.

5. Do you take time to listen?

Communication doesn't happen by itself. You must plan for it and spend both quality time and quantity time doing it. If you don't have time for your mate and your children, you are too busy. C.R. Lawton said, "Time is the one thing that can never be retrieved. One may lose and regain a friend; one may lose and regain money; opportunity spurned may come again; but the hours that are lost in idleness can never be brought back to be used in gainful pursuits." And time spent listening to our mates and our children is time well spent.

Understanding

While vacationing in Mexico some time ago we went into a neighborhood restaurant for dinner. Our waiter didn't speak English very well, but he wrote our order on his pad, then looked us in the eye and said, "Si." We were sure he understood our order because of his affirmative response. However, when he returned with our dinner—or what he thought we had ordered for dinner—we couldn't help but laugh at the missed communication.

We may speak clearly and our mates may listen intently, but if they don't understand the message, we haven't communicated very well. There are two major reasons why we fail to communicate this way. First, often there is a difference between what we mean to say and what we really say. The ideas may be clear in our heads, but the words we choose to express them aren't adequate. Second, sometimes there's a difference between what we hear and what we think we hear. We wrongly interpret what we've heard. And every time we respond to what we *think* we heard instead of what was actually said, the communication problem is further compounded.

One way to avoid communication problems is to repeat to your mate what you heard and then ask, "Is that what you said?" Whenever you ask that clarifying question you are helping to keep the channels of understanding wide open and flowing. It's important to communicate clearly.

HOW TO COMMUNICATE BETTER

In her book *After Every Wedding Comes a Marriage*, Florence Littauer reviews what men and women are looking for in communication. Being aware of your mate's general needs in this area will help you better communicate with him.

According to Littauer, men want four things: 1) *Sincerity:* They want to know that the topic is important to you; 2) *Simplicity:* They want to hear the simple facts and get to the point; 3) *Sensitivity:* They will open up better at the right time and the right place; and 4) *Stability:* They want to keep their composure and not fall apart during communication.

Women have four different wants: 1) *Attention:* They want their mate's full attention when they speak; 2) *Agreement:* They want no arguments to break down the walls between them and their mates; 3) *Appreciation:* They want their mates to value them and their roles; and 4) *Appointments:* They want their mates to honor the time and place for communication.[60]

Let me share a few additional tips that Emilie and I have successfully applied to our communication as husband and wife:

1. *Be willing to change.*

If you have been guilty of hindering communication in your

Keys to Listening with Love

- Listen intentionally
- Plan ahead
- Maintain eye-contact
- Ask questions
- Listen understandingly
- Don't interrupt
- Be patient
- Practice
- Consider the context
- Listen actively

—BECKY FREEMAN

family, you are not locked into that behavior. Ask God and your family members to forgive you for your failure. Then learn from your mistakes and change your communication pattern.

2. *It's okay to disagree.*

Always maintain respect and honor your mate when communicating your differences. Don't belittle, slander, or attack your partner, even in a heated exchange. You can disagree, but you also need to respect your spouse's opinions.

3. *It takes effort to communicate well.*

When you decide to communicate better, be aware that your decision is only the beginning. It takes a lot of effort and practice to become a good communicator. Communication is a matter of will and work.

4. *Don't second guess your partner.*

Sit on your hands, keep your mouth shut, and hear your partner out—even if it takes several hours for him to explain his point.

Solving Communication Breakdowns

There are many reasons for a communication breakdown between partners, perhaps as many reasons as there are couples. But there are several common problems that afflict couples. Do you recognize some familiar communication problems in your marriage from the list of statements below?

- I know my opinion doesn't matter to you.

Expressions of Love

- Evaluate your calendar. Make sure you have plenty of time for your husband.
- Give him 30 minutes to unwind before you talk about today's happenings.
- Give your husband a "care package" filled with his favorite snacks.
- Ask him to tell you about a time he enjoyed as a child.
- Have him tell you his favorite joke.

- I am afraid of your reaction.
- I talk so much that you stop listening.
- I know you will correct me or say I'm wrong.
- I get too depressed to talk sometimes.
- I get angry too easily when we talk.
- I don't like serious conversations so I make jokes when we talk.
- I am afraid of the silence between us.
- I don't like it when you interrupt me.
- I am afraid we won't agree.
- I am afraid you will make fun of me or my ideas.
- I always feel defensive when we talk.

If you and your mate want to prevent or repair communication breakdowns, you must identify the problem areas and plan a program to overcome them. In some cases the barriers to communication may be so great that you might need to seek out a trusted friend or Christian counselor.

Following the model below, create a list of your real or potential communication barriers. Then determine some actions you can take that will prevent or repair each problem. Write them down to help you put them into practice.

Communication Problems:	*Problem:* I am afraid of your reaction
Actions for Improvement:	*Response:* Take the risk to pray about my approach. Choose the right time and share how I feel when he/she talks about a difficult situation.

Christian marriage and family counselor Norm Wright says that many of us don't communicate because we don't believe that Christ accepts us as we are. Since we don't feel accepted by Christ, we don't accept ourselves, which means we can't accept others and communicate with them. We are too busy trying to shape up for God so that He will love us and accept us.[61]

The good news, of course, is that God has already accepted us because of our relationship with Jesus Christ. We don't need to prove anything to Him. We simply need to accept and reflect His love, which will help us accept ourselves and others. This opens all the doors that lead to good communication. The closer you each get to God, the closer you can get to each other!

Real Love Is

- Rational
- Not a single, easy act
- Costly
- Giving it first
- Best for those you love
- Not an uncontrollable feeling
- Not a warm puppy
- Not produced by trying to set it
- A choice followed by action
- A learned act
- Controlled by the will and leads to action
- Learned through reading God's word
- Affirmation to the one you love
- Recognizing the uniqueness of the loved one

What Makes a Man Feel Loved

14

A Love Song

Like an apple tree among the trees of the forest
is my lover among the young men.
I delight to sit in his shade,
and his fruit is sweet to my taste.
—Song of Solomon 2:3 (niv)

In our culture love is often equated with physical attraction, sexual feelings, and the act of intercourse. Love in this narrow context is selfish, mainly desiring that the love object meet personal needs. But love in the Scriptures involves attitudes and actions that are aimed at meeting your mate's needs irrespective of your personal feelings.

In his book *The Measure of a Marriage*, Gene Getz defines three Greek words that encompass the selfless three-dimensional love which should be present in our marriages:

> *Eros love*. Eros refers to sexual love. Though the word is not found in the New Testament, it was used during New Testament times to describe sexual activity which was based on selfish, sensual, erotic lovemaking. It's the kind of love most frequently displayed in today's movies, books, and magazines. Eros always involves a sexual response.

Christians may not feel that eros has a place in the sanctity of a Christian marriage. But erotic experiences, within the bounds of faithfulness to one's spouse, are an important part of marital love. For the Christian, erotic lovemaking must always be expressed within the boundaries of agape and phileo.

Phileo love. Phileo love refers to love that is emotionally positive in nature. It reflects true friendship, delight, and pleasure in a relationship. Romans 12:10 states that we are to be devoted to one another in brotherly love. Phileo describes the type of loving relationship which exists among family members: devotion, support, commitment, affection. Phileo is the dimension of love which involves responding to someone's needs affectionately and with positive emotions. Husbands and wives must learn to be devoted friends as well as lovers. . . .

The Eskimos have fifty-two names for snow because snow was important to them: there ought to be as many for love.

— MARGARET ATWOOD

Agape love. Agape is the most common word for love in the New Testament. It is love which actively seeks to do the right thing for, and meet the needs of, the love object. It is love which sacrifices personal feelings and needs to meet the needs of the spouse. In agape we willingly give up our rights, our desires, and our demands to fulfill our partners'. You may come home from work too tired to be kind or romantic to a spouse who needs your loving attention. But agape loves beyond what we feel like doing. Agape patiently seeks to discover and meet the needs of the other no matter what the personal cost may be.[62]

Our goal as Christians is to allow agape love to penetrate and rule the other two dimensions of love in our lives. In order to allow agape its rightful place, you must first know Jesus Christ as personal Savior, then be submissive to your spouse.

If you haven't made these basic commitments, you cannot move beyond eros and phileo love. Many marriages can survive on these two dimensions of love alone, but it is God's will for Christians to allow agape love to dominate all their relationships, especially marriage.

Song of Solomon

A dynamic book in the Bible gives us the pattern of married love as God intended it to be. The Song of Solomon's revelation is in such detail that it can serve as a guide and model for our own marriages. (The Song of Solomon is also known as the Song of Songs.)

This story is about the marriage between the king of Israel and a very lovely, naive country girl whom he met in the vineyards of his kingdom. This true-to-life episode dealing with real-life situations was written down through the inspiration of the Holy Spirit. Three-thousand years later we still read it and sense that our marriages truly please and honor God.

Many first-time readers will be surprised to find such vivid expressions of love in the Bible. You'll also be amazed at the broad range of practical insights to be gleaned from this book of Scripture. Biblical principles transcend time and cultural differences; Song of Solomon captures beautifully the poetry of love between a man and a woman.

Historians over the years have disagreed about what this book is attempting to teach the church. Some argue that it

---

Expressions of Love

- What is the most cherished memory you share with your mate? Relive it with him.
- What about your mate sparks your romantic interest? Let him know!
- Tell your man that you need him. Be prepared to give an example.
- Recreate the most romantic experience you ever shared with your mate.
- Register for a couples' retreat.

---

talks about love and marriage; others believe it is referring to Jesus Christ and His love for us. I believe both arguments are valid since Christian marriage is a reflection of Christ's love for His church. Ephesians 5:25 says, "Husbands, love your wives, just as Christ also loved the church and gave Himself up for her." (By the way, the woman is referred to as "Shulammite" [NIV]. Whether this is her name or her nationality doesn't matter. We can learn a lot from this woman.)

God's design for purity in love and marriage has always been at odds with the world's ideas. Whereas Scripture portrays marriage as a model representing Jesus Christ's relationship with the church, the world looks upon sex as a means of pleasure. The people indulge in sex, but they can't comprehend the idea of holiness and purity in the sexual relationship. Solomon teaches us the truth that romantic love is God's gift to us in marriage.

Characteristics of True Love: Love is patient, love is kind. It does not envy, it does not boast, it is not proud. It is not rude, it is not self-seeking, it is not easily angered, it keeps no record of wrongs. Love does not delight in evil but rejoices with the truth. It always protects, always trusts, always hopes, always perseveres.

—1 CORINTHIANS 13:4-7

In Song of Solomon we find a vineyard maiden tanned by the hot sun of the fields being courted by the king of Israel. She felt inferior to the light-skinned maidens of Solomon's court, and she thought she was unworthy to be his queen. But Solomon, in all of his wisdom, was able to build up her self image. He praised her every opportunity he could. He lifted her up; he voiced appreciation of her physical appearance; he compared her with all the other women and found none other more attractive and inviting. She was flawless and perfect in his eyes. He not only did this in courtship but all through their marriage. We need to learn this principle of giving praise to our mates. Both husbands and wives need to hear praise!

Not only did Solomon praise his wife, he also was not found to criticize her. One of Emilie's and my favorite verses is found in Ephesians 4:29 which reads, "Do not let any unwholesome talk come out of your mouths, but only what is helpful for building others up according to their needs, that it may benefit those who listen" (NIV). Never in this book does Solomon utter one word of criticism. His words are always positive and uplifting. This consideration bore much fruit and blessings in their marriage. By his praise, Solomon let everyone know that he loved his wife more than anything in the whole kingdom. As Solomon treated her as a queen she became just that—a queen. Isn't it amazing how we become how we are treated and respected!

In the following paraphrase by S. Craig Glickman, the love and affection found in the Song of Solomon is clearly developed. Notice how this couple built their love for each other in both physical and emotional ways. Share this interpretative paraphrase with your husband! You'll discover how the love between a husband and wife is blessed by God and is a form of worship to Him.

May God richly bless you as you read this interpretation of the Song of Solomon.[63]

The Most Beautiful Love Song Ever Written
Song of Solomon

Shulamith's First Days in the Palace (1:2-11)

The King's fiancee, Shulamith, in soliloquy: How I wish he would shower me with kisses, for his exquisite kisses are more desirable than the finest wine. The gentle fragrance of your cologne brings the enchantment of springtime. Yes, it is the rich fragrance of your heart that awakens my love and respect. Yes, it is your character that brings you admiration from every girl of the court. How I long for you to come take me with you to run and laugh through the countryside of this kingdom. (You see, the King had brought me to the kingdom's palace.)

Women of the court to the King: We will always be very thankful and happy because of you, O King. For we love to speak of the inspiring beauty of your love.

Shulamith in soliloquy: They rightly love a person like you, my King.

Shulamith to women of the court: I realize that I do not display the fair and delicate skin of one raised in the comfort of a palace. I am darkened from the sun—indeed, as dark as the tents of the humble nomads I used to work beside. But now I might say that I am also as dark as the luxurious drapery of the King's palace. Nevertheless, what loveliness I do have is not so weak that the gaze of the sun should make it bow its head in shame. And if the glare of the sun could not shame me, please know that neither will the glare of your contempt. I could not help it that my stepbrothers were angry with me and demanded that I work in the vineyard they had leased from the King. It was possible for me to care for it and for the vineyard of my own appearance.

Shulamith to King: Please tell me, whom I love so deeply, where you take your royal flock for its afternoon rest. I don't want to search randomly for you, wandering about like a woman of the streets.

Women of the court to Shulamith: If you do not know, O fairest among women, why not simply go ahead and follow the trail of the flocks, and then pasture your flock beside the shepherd's huts?

King to Shulamith: Your presence captivates attention as thoroughly as a single mare among a hundred stallions. And how perfectly your lovely jewelry and necklace adorn your lovely face.

Women of the court to Shulamith: We shall make even more elegant necklaces of gold and silver to adorn her face.

In a Palace Room (1:12-14)

Shulamith in soliloquy: While my King was dining at his table, my perfume refreshed me with its soothing fragrance. For my King is the fragrance and my thoughts of him are like a sachet of perfume hung around my neck, over my heart, continually refreshing me. How dear he is to me, as dear as the delicate henna blossoms in the oasis of En-Gedi. What joy I have found in that oasis!

In the Countryside (1:15–2:7)

King to Shulamith: You are so beautiful, my love. You are so beautiful. Your soft eyes are as gentle as doves.

Shulamith to King: And you are handsome, my love, and so enjoyable. It's so wonderful to walk through our home of nature together. Here the cool grass is a soft couch to lie upon, to catch our breath and to gaze at the beams and rafters of our house—the towering cedars and cypresses all around. Lying here I feel like a rose from the valley of Sharon, the loveliest flower in the valley.

King to Shulamith: Only the loveliest flower in the valley? No, my love. To me you are like a flower among thorns compared with any other woman in the world.

Shulamith to King: And you, my precious King, are like a fruitful apple tree among the barren trees of the forest compared with all the men in the world.

Shulamith in soliloquy: No longer do I labor in the heat of the sun. I find cool rest in the shade of this apple tree. Nourishment from its magical fruit brings me the radiant health only love brings. And he loves me so much. Even when he brings me to the great royal banquets attended by the most influential people in this kingdom and beyond, he is never so concerned for them that his love and his care for me is not as plain as a royal banner lifted high above my head. How dear he is to me! My delightful peace in his love makes me so weak from joy that I must rest in his arms for strength. Yet such loving comfort makes me more joyful and weaker still. How I wish he could lay me down beside him and embrace me! But how important it is I promise, with the gentle gazelles and deer of the countryside as my witnesses, not to attempt to awaken love until love is pleased to awaken itself.

On the Way to the Countryside (2:8-17)

Shulamith in soliloquy: I hear my beloved. Look! He is coming to visit. And he is as dashing as a young stag leaping upon the mountains, springing upon the hills. There he is, standing at the door, trying to peer through the window and peep through the lattice. At last he speaks.

King to Shulamith: Come, my darling, my fair one, come with me. For look, the winter has passed. The rain is over and gone. The blossoms have appeared in the land. The time of singing has come, and the voice of the turtledove has been heard in the land. The fig tree has ripened its figs, and the vines in blossom have given forth fragrance. Let us go, my darling, my lovely one; come along with me. O my precious, gentle dove. You have been like a dove in the clefts of the mountain rocks, in the hidden places along the mountain trails. Now come out from the hidden place and let me see you. Let me hear the coo of your voice. For your voice is sweet and you are as gracefully beautiful as a dove in flight silhouetted against a soft blue sky. My love, what we have together is a valuable treasure; it is like a garden of the loveliest flowers in the world. Let us promise each other to catch any foxes that could spoil our garden when now at long last it blossoms for us.

Shulamith in soliloquy: My beloved belongs to me and I belong to him—this tender King who grazes his flock among the lilies.

Shulamith to the King: How I long for the time when all through the night, until the day takes its first breath and the morning shadows flee from the sun, that you, my beloved King, might be a gazelle upon the hills of my breasts.

Shulamith Waits for Her Fiancé (3:1-5)

Shulamith in soliloquy: How I miss the one I love so deeply. I could not wait to see him. I thought to myself, "I must get up and find him. I will get up now and look around the streets and squares of the city for him. Surely I'll be able to find this one I love so much." But I could not find him. When the night watchmen of the city found me, I immediately asked them if they had seen this one I loved so deeply. But they had not. Yet no sooner did I pass from them than I found my beloved. I held on and on and would not let him go until I could bring him to my home. I still held on until my fearful anxieties left me and I felt peaceful once again. How hard it is to be patient! You women of the court, we must promise ourselves, by the gazelles and deer of the field, not to awaken love until love is pleased to awaken itself.

The Wedding Day (3:6-11)

Poet: What can this be coming from the outskirts of the city like columns of smoke, perfumed clouds of myrrh and frankincense, clouds of the scented powders of the merchant? Look! It is the royal procession with Solomon carried upon his lavish couch by his strongest servants. And take a look at all those soldiers around it! That is the imperial guard, the sixty mightiest warriors in the entire kingdom. Each one is an expert with his weapon and valiant in battle. Yet now each one has a sword at his side only for the protection of the King and his bride. Look at the luxurious couch Solomon is carried on. He has had it made especially for this day. He made its frame from the best timber of Lebanon. Its posts are made of silver, its back of gold, and its seat of royal purple cloth. And do you see its delicate craftsmanship! It reflects the skill of the women of the court who gave their best work out of love for the King and his bride. Let us all go out and look upon King Solomon wearing his elegant wedding crown. Let us go out and see him on the most joyful day of his life.

The Wedding Night (4:1–5:1)

King to Shulamith: You are so beautiful my love, you are so beautiful. Your soft eyes are as gentle as doves from behind your wedding veil. Your hair is as captivating as the flowing movement of a flock descending a mountain at sunset. Your full and lovely smile is as cheerful and sparkling as pairs of young lambs scurrying up from a washing. And only a thread of scarlet could have outlined your lips so perfectly. Your cheeks flush with the redness of the pomegranate's hue. Yet you walk with dignity and stand with the strength of a fortress. Your necklace sparkles like the shields upon the fortress tower. But your breasts are as soft and gentle as fawns grazing among lilies. And now at last, all through the night—until the day takes its first breath and the morning shadows flee from the sun—I will be a gazelle upon the hills of your perfumed breasts. You are completely and perfectly beautiful, my love, and flawless in every way. Now bring your thoughts completely to me, my love. Leave your fears in the far away mountains and rest in the security of my arms. You excite me, my darling bride; you excite me with but a glance of your eyes, with but a strand of your necklace. How wonderful are your caresses, my beloved bride. Your love is more sweetly intoxicating than the finest wine. And the fragrance of your perfume is better than the finest spices. The richness of honey and milk is under your tongue, my love. And the fragrance of your garments is like the fragrance of the forests of Lebanon. You are a beautiful garden fashioned only for me, my darling bride. Yes, like a garden kept only for me. Or like a fresh fountain sealed just for me. Your garden is overflowing with beautiful and delicate flowers of every scent and color. It is a paradise of pomegranates with luscious fruit, with henna blossoms and nard, nard and saffron, calamus and cinnamon with trees of frankincense, myrrh and aloes with all the choicest of spices. And you are pure as fresh water, yet more than a mere fountain. You are a spring for many gardens—a well of life-giving water. No, even more, you are like the fresh streams flowing from Lebanon which give life to the entire countryside.

Shulamith to King: Awake, O north wind, and come, wind of the south. Let your breezes blow upon my garden and carry its fragrant spices to my beloved. May he follow the enchanting spices to my garden and come in to enjoy its luscious fruit.

King to Shulamith: I have rejoiced in the richness of your garden, my darling bride. I have been intoxicated by the fragrance of your myrrh and perfume. I have tasted the sweetness of your love like honey. I have enjoyed the sweetness of your love like an exquisite wine and the refreshment of your love like the coolness of milk.

Poet to couple: Rejoice in your lovemaking as you would rejoice at a great feast, O lovers. Eat and drink from this feast to the fullest. Drink, drink and be drunk with one another's love.

Shulamith in soliloquy: I was half asleep when I heard the sound of my beloved husband knocking gently upon the door of our palace chamber. He whispered softly, "I'm back from the countryside, my love, my darling, my perfect wife." My only answer was a mumbled, "I've already gone to sleep, my dear." After all, I had already prepared for bed. I had washed my face and put on my old nightgown. But then my beloved gently opened the door and I realized I really wanted to see him. I had hesitated too long though. By the time I arose to open the door, he had already walked away, leaving only a gift of my favorite perfume as a reminder of his love for me. Deep within my heart I was reawakened to my love for him. It was just that the fatigue and distractions of the day had brought my hesitating response. I decided to try to find him. I threw on my clothes, went outside the palace and began to call out to him. But things went from bad to worse. The nightwatchmen of the city mistook me for a secretive criminal sneaking about in the night. They arrested me in their customarily rough style, then jerking my shawl from my head they saw the face of their newly found suspect—a "great" police force we have! O, you women of the court, if you see my beloved King, please tell him that I deeply love him, that I am lovesick for him.

Women of the court to Shulamith: What makes your husband better than any other, O fairest of women? What makes him so great that you request this so fervently of us?

Shulamith to women of the court: My beloved husband is strikingly handsome, the first to be noticed among ten thousand men. When I look at him, I see a face with a tan more richly golden than gold itself. His hair is as black as a raven's feathers and as lovely as palm leaves atop the stately palm tree. When I look into his eyes, they are as gentle as doves peacefully resting by streams of water. They are as pure and clear as health can make them. When he places his cheek next to mine, it is as fragrant as a garden of perfumed flowers. His soft lips are as sweet and scented as lilies dripping with nectar. And how tender are his fingers like golden velvet when he touches me! He is a picture of strength and vitality. His stomach is as firm as a plate of ivory rippling with sapphires. And his legs are as strong and elegant as alabaster pillars set upon pedestals of fine gold. His appearance is like majestic Mt. Lebanon, prominent with its towering cedars. But beyond this, the words of his heart are full of charm and delight. He is completely wonderful in every way. This is the one I love so deeply, and this is the one who is my closest friend, O women of the palace court.

Women of the court to Shulamith: Where has your beloved gone, then, O fairest among women? Where has he gone? We will help you find him.

Shulamith to women of the court: Oh, I know him well enough to know where he has gone. He likes to contemplate as he walks through the garden and cares for his special little flock among the lilies. I know him, for I belong to him and he belongs to me—this gentle shepherd who pastures his flock among the lilies.

THE PROBLEM RESOLVED (6:4-13)

King to Shulamith: My darling, did you know that you are as lovely as the city of Tirzah glittering on the horizon of night? No, more than that you are as lovely as the fair city of Jerusalem. Your beauty is as breathtaking as scores of marching warriors. (No, do not look at me like that now, my love; I have more to tell you.) Do you remember what I said on our wedding night? It is still just as true. Your hair is as captivating as the flowing movement of a flock descending a mountain at sunset. Your lovely smile is as cheerful and sparkling as pairs of young lambs scurrying up from a washing. And your cheeks still flush with the redness of the pomegranate's hue.

King in soliloquy: The palace is full of its aristocratic ladies and dazzling mistresses belonging to the noblemen of the court. But my lovely wife, my dove, my flawless one, is unique among them all. And these ladies and mistresses realize it too. They too must praise her. As we approached them in my chariot, they eventually perceived that we were together again.

Women of the court to one another: Who is that on the horizon like the dawn, now fair as the moon but now plain and bright as the sun and as majestic as scores of marching warriors?

Shulamith in the chariot in soliloquy: I went down to the garden where I knew my King would be. I wanted to see if the fresh flowers and fruits of spring had come. I wanted to see if our reunion might bring a new season of spring love for my husband and me. Before I knew what happened, we were together again and riding past the palace court in his chariot. I can still hear them calling out, "Return, return O Shulamith; return that we may gaze at the beloved wife of the King.

King to Shulamith: How they love to look upon the incomparable grace and beauty of a queen.

In the Royal Bedroom (7:1-10)

King to Shulamith: How delicate are your feet in sandals, my royal prince's daughter! The curves of your hips are as smooth and graceful as the curves of elegant jewelry, perfectly fashioned by the skillful hands of a master artist. As delectable as a feast of wine and bread is your stomach—your navel is like the goblet of wine, and your stomach is the soft warm bread. Your breasts are as soft and gentle as fawns grazing among the lilies, twins of a gazelle, and your neck is smooth as ivory to the touch. Your eyes are as peaceful as the pools of water in the valley of Heshbon, near the gates of the populous city. Yet how strong you walk in wisdom and discretion. You are indeed as majestically beautiful as Mt Carmel. Your long flowing hair is as cool and soft as silken threads draped round my neck, yet strong enough to bind me as your captive forever. How lovely and delightful you are, my dear, and how especially delightful is your love! You are as graceful and splendorous as a palm tree silhouetted against the sky. Yes, a palm tree—and your breasts are its luscious fruit. I think I shall climb my precious palm tree and take its tender fruit gently into my hand. O my precious one, let your breasts be like the tender fruit to my taste, and now let me kiss you and breathe your fragrant breath. Let me kiss you and taste a sweetness better than wine.

Shulamith to King: And savor every drop, my lover, and let its sweetness linger long upon your lips, and let every drop of this wine bring a peaceful sleep.

Shulamith in soliloquy: I belong to my beloved husband and he loves me from the depths of his soul.

In the Countryside (7:11–8:14)

Shulamith to King: Spring's magic flowers have perfumed the pastel countryside and enchanted the hearts of all lovers. Come, my precious lover; every delicious fruit of spring is ours for the taking. Let us return to our springtime cottage of towering cedars and cypresses where the plush green grass is its endless carpet and the orchids are its shelves for every luscious fruit. I have prepared a basketful for you, my love, to give you in a sumptuous banquet of love beneath the sky. I wish we could pretend you were my brother, my real little brother. I could take you outside to play, and playfully kiss you whenever I wished. But then I could also take your hand and bring you inside and you could teach me and share with me your deep understanding of life. Then how I wish you would lay me down beside you and love me.

Shulamith to women of the court: I encourage you not to try to awaken love until love is pleased to awaken itself. How wonderful it is when it blossoms in the proper season.

Shulamith to King: Do you remember where our love began? Under the legendary sweetheart tree, of course, where every love begins and grows and then brings forth a newborn child, yet not without the pain of birth. Neither did our love begin without the pain, the fruitful pain of birth. O, my darling lover, make me your most precious possession held securely in your arms, held close to your heart. True love is as strong and irreversible as the onward march of death. True love never ceases to care, and it would no more give up the beloved than the grave would give up the dead. The fires of true love can never be quenched because the source of its flame is God himself. Even were a river of rushing water to pass over it, the flame would yet shine forth. Of all the gifts in the world, this priceless love is the most precious and possessed only by those to whom it is freely given. For no man could purchase it with money, even the richest man in the world.

King to Shulamith: Do you remember how it was given to us?

Shulamith to King: My love, I truly believe I was being prepared for it long before I even dreamed of romance. I remember hearing my brothers talking one evening. It was shortly after my father died, and they were concerned to raise me properly, to prepare me for the distant day of marriage. They were like a roomful of fathers debating about what to do with their only daughter. They finally resolved simply to punish and restrict me if I were promiscuous but to reward and encourage me if I were chaste. How thankful I am that I made it easy for them. I could see even when I was very young that I wanted to keep myself for the one dearest man in my life. And then you came. And everything I ever wanted I found in you. There I was, working daily in the vineyard my brothers had leased from you. And you "happened" to pass by and see me. That's how our love began. I remember when I worked in that vineyard that a thousand dollars went to you and two hundred dollars for the ones taking care of its fruit for you. Now I am your vineyard, my lover, and I gladly give the entire thousand dollars of my worth to you; I give myself completely, withholding nothing of my trust, my thoughts, my care, my love. But my dear King, let us not forget that two hundred dollars belongs to the ones who took care of the fruit of my vineyard for you. How thankful we must be to my family who helped prepare me for you.

King to Shulamith: My darling, whose home is the fragrant garden, everyone listens for the sound of your voice, but let me alone hear it now.

Shulamith to King: Hurry, then, my beloved. And again be like a gazelle or young stag on the hills of my perfumed breasts.

God is the love of our lives, and He has called us in accordance with His purpose; therefore He has promised us that all things will work together today for our good.

—Adapted from Romans 8:28

15

Some Concluding Thoughts

The husband is the head of the wife, as Christ also is the head of the church, He Himself being the Savior of the body. But as the church is subject to Christ, so also the wives ought to be to their husbands in everything. Husbands, love your wives, just as Christ also loved the church and gave Himself up for her.

—Ephesians 5:23-25

As I close this book, I am reminded of something my dear friend Bill Thornburgh said when he faced his third bout with cancer, and chemotherapy was no longer a possibility. His doctor told him, "Bill, go home and have a wonderful August and I will see you again in September." At the same time Bill shared his doctor's words with me, he told me he was going to write a book called *My Shrinking World*. Together, the doctor's words and the title of Bill's book have a message for all of us.

Not one of us knows if we're living through August, and none of us knows whether we'll see September. And few of us are aware of how our world may be shrinking. We don't know how much time we have, so we need to cherish each day God gives us with our spouse. So I challenge you to enjoy the time you have with your husband.

My prayer for you is that your August will blossom into a wonderful September and into many other wonderful months. My prayer for you is that your world, which may seem to be shrinking and crowding in around you, will open up so that you can clearly see God's perfect will for your life and experience His will for your marriage.

How Will You Respond?

Stand by your man! We are desperately in need of women who honor and respect the commitment they made to God and to their husbands. (However, if you're in an abusive situation, don't stay.) Make sure you and your children are safe. If you are discouraged, impatient, confused, or disappointed, don't throw away a diamond in the rough. I challenge you to work to make your marriage the kind of relationship that God designed it to be—a relationship that reflects Christ's love for the church and the church's devotion to its Savior.

I hope you have come to understand more clearly the pressures, the challenges, and the needs of your man. Now let me take one final risk and share for your husband the following words—words that he may want to speak but, for whatever reasons, is unable to share with you right now.

> *My dearest wife . . .*
>
> Thank you for choosing me to share your life with you. Thank you for your honesty and transparency. I know it can be painful at times.
>
> Deep down inside I really know that you love me. But I'm a man and I need tangible reminders of your love. There is very little of this life of greater value to me than your love. I need it. I need you.

Could I ask you a favor? I love to receive letters from you, but I don't ever want to ask for them—it takes the fun out of receiving them if it's my idea. But would you write me a letter?

I need to know:

- how you appreciate me . . .
- what I've done to show that I respect you . . .
- how I've been an encouragement to you . . .
- that you appreciate the "little things" I do every week for you . . .
- of your unconditional acceptance of me, just as I am . . .
- how I am a partner to you . . .
- why you enjoy me . . .
- how I've changed for good or ways that you've seen me grow (I forget sometimes) . . .
- that you want to meet my needs . . .
- that your love will persevere . . .

You can write it any way you'd like, but please tell me. I really do love you.

I love you,

Your husband

P.S. I'm not perfect either, but I'm glad we're in this thing together.[64]

Be a Risk-Taker

I know that meeting that challenge calls you to take the risk of being open, honest, and transparent—and that it makes you vulnerable to being laughed at, ignored, or rejected. Even within a marriage taking this kind of risk may be very threatening, but taking that risk is better than the alternative of shriveling up and dying as a couple. Perhaps the following thoughts will encourage you to take the risk of finding new intimacy and, therefore, new delight in your marriage.

> To laugh is to appear the fool.
> To weep is to risk appearing sentimental.
> To reach out for another is to risk involvement.
> To expose feelings is to risk exposing your true self.
> To place your ideas, your dreams, before the crowd
> is to risk their loss.
> To love is to risk not being loved in return.
> To live is to risk dying.
> To hope is to risk despair.
> To try is to risk failure.
> But risks must be taken, because the greatest
> hazard in life is to risk nothing.
> The person who risks nothing, does nothing, has
> nothing, and is nothing.
> He may avoid suffering and sorrow.
> But he simply cannot learn, feel, change, grow,
> love and live.
> Chained by his certitudes, he is a slave.
> He has forfeited freedom.
> Only a person who risks is free![65]

Take the risk of standing by your man. You really do have much to gain!

- ♥ Show [your husband] in a thousand little ways that you love him and think he's a wonderful person. Romance dies through indifference and neglect. You can keep it alive by being a responsive lover, by looking attractive, and by using some of the feminine ways that God has given you.
- ♥ Remember that a man also needs appreciation and compliments. If he gets it from his wife, he's far less likely to look for it elsewhere.
- ♥ Make your husband feel you're the one person in the world whom he can always rely on for sympathy and understanding. Earn his confidence by keeping his secrets.

Rejoice in his triumphs and sympathize with his defeats. Don't belittle his accomplishments or laugh at his mistakes.

- ♥ Interest yourself in things that interest him so you can enjoy them together. When you share many interests, you get keener pleasures from each other's company and have endless topics for conversation.

- ♥ Take care of your share of the domestic load. This means keeping the home clean and attractive, being a good cook and a thrifty shopper. It means being cheerful even when times are hard and encouraging him when he is losing faith in himself. It means doing all you can do to help him get ahead by discussing his business problems with him and making friends for him.

- ♥ Keep your husband amused and entertained, and be ready to go out "on the town" when he's in the mood. Many men seek outside recreation alone because their wife is too busy with household details or other interests, or because she is too dull to provide an evening's diversion. Other men go out alone because their mates are "kill joys" or "worry warts."

- ♥ The impression people get of your man will depend largely on what you say about him and how you act toward him in public. Don't play the martyr, looking for sympathy at the expense of your husband. As you make only favorable remarks about him and act as if he's a fine person, you'll be helping him as well as yourself.

- ♥ No matter how old your husband is, he still needs to be babied and cuddled once in a while. He needs to be watched and worried over when he's ill.[66]

Do some of those ideas sound familiar even though they were first broadcast over 46 years ago? Do they remind you that you are not alone in the challenges you face being a wife? Do they encourage you to reach out to your man—whatever the risk?

THE BATTLE CRY

As I've said throughout the book—support and encourage your man! Stand by your God—by your commitment to Him and the commitment to your husband you made before Him. Be sensitive to your man's needs. Be willing to meet them. Understand how he is different from you and realize that different doesn't mean superior or inferior. Be your husband's best friend. Stand with him when his decisions don't work out and when his heart is hard toward God . . . and even toward you. Support his work and encourage him to be confident and strong in this society that is confused about masculinity.

Yes, it's a tall order, but I'm sure no one ever told you that marriage would be easy. Know that in the strength of the Lord and with the guidance of His Word, you can indeed meet the challenges and stand by your man—regardless of your circumstances.

Gifts Nobody Returns

- Praise for a job well done.
- Consideration—offering to walk in another man's shoes.
- Gratitude—a word, a note, a smile with meaning in it.
- Inspiration—being what you want another to be.
- An offer—to share a bit of your time, your heart, and your love willingly, behaving as if it no longer belongs to you.

— ANONYMOUS

NOTES

1. These ten lies are quoted from and the discussion of them based on pp. 3-10 from Dr. Toni Grant's *Being a Woman* (New York: Random House, 1988). Used by permission.
2. "Barbara Bush Chided at Wellesley College," *Los Angeles Times*, June 2, 1990.
3. "The Best Advice I Ever Heard," *Press Enterprise* (Riverside, CA), May 12, 1991.
4. Larry Crabb, *The Marriage Builder* (Grand Rapids, MI: Zondervan, 1982), pp. 105-06.
5. Dennis and Barbara Rainey, *Building Your Mate's Self Esteem* (San Bernadino, CA: Here's Life Publishers, 1986), pp. 74-75.
6. Bill Hybels, *Honest to God* (Grand Rapids, MI: Zondervan, 1990), pp. 53-54.
7. H. Norman Wright, *Quiet Times for Couples* (Eugene, OR: Harvest House Publishers, 1990), p. 35.
8. Robert Fulghum, *All I Really Need to Know I Learned in Kindergarten* (New York: Ballantine Books, 1986), pp. 29-31.
9. Ibid., p. 31.
10. H. Norman Wright, *Making Peace with Your Partner* (Waco, TX: Word Books, 1988), adapted from pp. 173-74.
11. Mordecai L. Brill, Marlene Halpin, and William H. Genne, eds., *Writing Your Own Wedding* (Chicago: Follett, 1979), p. 88.
12. For more information on this subject, you might want to read Emilie Barnes, *The Spirit of Loveliness* (Eugene, OR: Harvest House Publishers, 1992).
13. Toni Grant, *Being a Woman* (New York: Random House, 1988), p. 55.

14. Ibid., p. 98.
15. Charles R. Swindoll, *Growing Strong in the Seasons of Life* (Portland, OR: Multnomah Press, 1983), p. 83.
16. Grant, *Being a Woman*, p. 46.
17. Grant, *Being a Woman*, pp. 68-69.
18. Willard F. Harley, Jr., *His Needs, Her Needs* (Tarrytown, NY: Fleming H. Revell, 1986), p. 10.
19. Ibid., p. 78.
20. These instructions are based on a detailed model from Harley, *His Needs, Her Needs*, pp. 130-35.
21. Joyce Brothers, *What Every Woman Should Know About Men*, (New York: Ballantine Books, 1981), p. 31.
22. Doreen Kimura, "Male Brain, Female Brain: The Hidden Difference," *Psychology Today*, November 1985, p. 56.
23. William and Nancy Carmichael with Dr. Timothy Boyd, *That Man! Understanding the Difference Between You and Your Husband* (Nashville: Thomas Nelson, 1988), adapted from chapter 2.
24. Adapted from Warren Farrell, *Why Men Are the Way They Are* (New York: McGraw-Hill, 1986), p. 139.
25. Carol Gilligan, *In a Different World* (Cambridge, MA: Harvard University Press, 1981), p. 8.
26. Mary Conroy, "Sexism in Our Schools: Training Girls for Failure?" *Better Homes and Gardens*, February 1988, pp. 44-48.
27. Carmichael, Carmichael, and Boyd, *That Man!* adapted from chapter 4.
28. For information on the Littauer's books and ministry write to: CLASS, 4508 Samara Rd., Albuquerque, NM 87120.
29. Harold J. Sala, *Today Can Be Different* (Ventura, CA: Regal Books, 1988), part of the devotional for July 6.
30. Larry Crabb, *The Marriage Builder* (Grand Rapids, MI: Zondervan, 1982), p. 22.
31. Florence Littauer, *After Every Wedding Comes a Marriage* (Eugene, OR: Harvest House, 1981), p. 22.
32. Fred and Florence Littauer, *Freeing Your Mind from the Memories That Bind* (San Bernardino, CA: Here's Life Publishers, 1988), pp. 27-30. Additional printed test sheets can be ordered from CLASS Speakers at 800-433-6633.

33. Florence Littauer, *Personalities in Power* (Lafayette, LA: Huntington House Inc., 1989), summaries from pp. 20-32.

34. Colleen and Louis Evans, Jr., *My Lover, My Friend* (Old Tappan, NJ: Fleming H. Revell, 1976), pp. 121-23.

35. Hybels, *Honest to God*, points adapted from pp. 101-04.

36. Alan Loy McGinnis, *The Friendship Factor* (Minneapolis, MN: Augsburg, 1979), p. 23.

37. Ibid., p. 9.

38. Jerry and Barbara Cook, *Choosing to Love* (Ventura, CA: Regal Books, 1982), pp. 78-80.

39. Marion Woodman, *Addiction to Perfection: The Unravished Bride* (Toronto: Inner City Books, 1982), p. 7.

40. Grant, *Being a Woman*, summarized from pp. 88-89.

41. Cook and Cook, *Choosing to Love*, pp. 18-19.

42. H. Norman Wright, *Quiet Times for Couples* (Eugene, OR: Harvest House Publishers, 1990), p. 35.

43. Source unknown.

44. *Los Angeles Times*, June 19, 1991.

45. Littauer and Littauer, *Freeing Your Mind*, adapted from pp. 31-35.

46. Hybels, *Honest to God*, p. 136.

47. Wright, *Quiet Times for Couples*, p. 57.

48. Donald R. Harvey, *The Drifting Marriage* (Old Tappan, NJ: Fleming H. Revell, 1988), p. 99.

49. Hybels, *Honest to God*, p. 31.

50. Grant, *Being a Woman*, pp. 96-97.

51. Roy Croft in Joan Winmill Brown and Bill Brown, *Together Each Day* (Old Tappan, NJ: Fleming H. Revell, 1940), p. 43.

52. Wright, *Quiet Times for Couples*, p. 357.

53. Florida Scott-Maxwell, *Women and Sometimes Men* (New York: Alfred Al Knopf, 1957), p. 47.

54. Gordon Dalbey, *Healing the Masculine Soul* (Waco, TX: Word Books, 1988), p. 53.

55. Source unknown.

56. H. Norman Wright, *Communication: Key to Your Marriage* (Regal Books, 1974), p. 52.

57. Adapted from Denis Waitley, *Seeds of Greatness* (Pocket Books, Division of Simon and Schuster, Inc., 1983), p. 160.
58. John Powell, *Why Am I Afraid to Tell You Who I Am?* (Argus Communications), adapted from pp. 54-62.
59. Florence Littauer, *After Every Wedding Comes a Marriage* (Eugene, OR: Harvest House Publishers, 1981), adapted from pp. 168-76.
60. Wright, *Communication*, adapted from pp. 71-79.
61. Gene Getz, *The Measure of a Marriage* (Regal Books, 1980), p. 114.
62. Taken from *A Song for Lovers* by S. Craig Glickman, © 1976 by InterVarsity Christian Fellowship of the USA. Used by permission of S. Craig Glickman.
63. Rainey and Rainey, *Building Your Mate's Self-Esteem*, adapted from p. 212.
64. Wright, *Quiet Times for Couples*, p. 18.
65. Samuel and Esther King, marriage counselors, gave this advice on Don McNeil's "Breakfast Club" show in 1951.

For more information regarding speaking engagements and additional material, please send a self-addressed stamped envelope to:

More Hours in My Day
2150 Whitestone Drive
Riverside, CA 92506